A Breath of Fresh Air

If adult Sunday School is vital, then we have no choice but to discover ways to move it into the 21st century as a living part of our mission. If it is merely excess baggage, the quicker we can jettison it the better. Most agree that the Church of the 21st century will need to be lean and focused. It will not be able to afford to drag unnecessary or counterproductive programs along with it.

A Breath of Fresh Air

*Christian Education of Adults
in the 21st Century*

by
Richard Lee Spindle

Beacon Hill Press of Kansas City
Kansas City, Missouri

ISBN: 083-411-3007

Printed in the
United States of America

Cover: Paul Franitza

Unless otherwise indicated, all scriptures are from *The Holy Bible, New International Version* (NIV), copyright © 1973, 1978, 1984 by the International Bible Society, and are used by permission.

Permission to quote from the following copyrighted version of the Scriptures is acknowledged with appreciation:

The *Revised Standard Version of the Bible* (RSV), copyrighted 1946, 1952, © 1971, 1973.

KJV—King James Version.

10   9   8   7   6   5   4   3   2   1

To my wife, Billy Lee, who lovingly and diligently
translated handwritten pages onto computer
disks.

To Rev. Robert B. Williams, a great pastor of his
present church for over 25 years, who gave
me the concept of "a breath of fresh air."

Contents

Introduction

What would happen if we lost the adult Sunday School in the 21st century? What difference would it make to the Church? More important, what difference would it make for the adults themselves? Is the adult Sunday School vital or is it excess baggage the Church has acquired through the years?

If adult Sunday School is vital, then we have no choice but to discover ways to move it into the 21st century as a living part of our mission. If it is merely excess baggage, the quicker we can jettison it the better. Most agree that the Church of the 21st century will need to be lean and focused. It will not be able to afford to drag unnecessary or counterproductive programs along with it.

Educating adults has been an integral part of my life for over 20 years. I have been concerned about *how adults learn* and *how teachers of adults teach.* I have tried to stay in touch with where adults are and what they are thinking and feeling. "Keeping in touch" has involved continuous teaching of adults in the local church and college classrooms, as well as the writing of curriculum, the developing of training material, and the training of teachers. For the last seven years, I have taught an adult Sunday School class in my local church.

I am intensely concerned about what is appearing to be a shaky future for the Christian education of adults in many of our churches. Some churches gave up on adults long ago. Other churches stopped stressing adult Sunday School more recently. Most of these churches are dying. We too will die unless we can discover effective ways to educate our people in the facts of the faith as we move into the 21st century.

Bishop Richard Wilke chronicles what is happening to the Sunday School in his United Methodist church. "Our denomination is now in its twentieth year of diminishing strength," he writes. "The decline of the church school began in 1960 and has continued precipitously ever since."[1] In 1964, 4.2 million people attended Methodist Sunday Schools. Twenty years later, in 1984, only 2.1 million were attending. Bishop Wilke laments, "Half of our church school is gone! Over 2 million people are no longer with us."[2] The Methodists also suffered the loss of 120,000 teachers and workers in that same 20-year span. What is becoming shockingly clear to us is that our world is rapidly becoming "adult"! If there ever was a time when the Christian education of adults ought to be healthy and functional, it is now and in the years leading into the new millennium. The "graying of America" is already being recognized by the marketplace. "Growing old" is now becoming fashionable. Recognizing this growing market of older persons, advertisers are "beginning to target what may be one of the primary consumer groups of the early 21st century."[3] This "graying of America" is also impacting the college campus. In a *Newsweek* magazine article titled "The Graying of the Campus," Connie Leslie writes:

> College town is turning gray. A new study by the College Board has found that 6 million students—45 percent of the nation's undergraduate and graduate enrollment—are at least 25 years old. Within ten years, the study projects that older students could constitute a majority on campus.[4]

And this aging of society will greatly impact the church.

We have an option. We can let the future happen to us, and then try to respond; or we can try to guide and shape what happens to us. John Stott, in his book *The Year 2000,* believes we are responsible to a great degree for what the church and her organizations and agencies become. He writes: "One of the distinctive characteristics of human beings, as Paolo Freire and others have argued, is that instead of history flowing over us, we are able (under God) to influence its course. We are responsible before God for the kind of society which develops."[5]

The purpose of this book, then, is to show that however new and different the 21st century may be, whatever cultural and global changes may or may not occur, the basic needs of adults *do not change.* Amid the confusions and complexities of a new millennium, adults will always be in need of "a breath of fresh air." The secret of our success with adults as we move toward the 21st century will be in proportion to our ability to provide creating, releasing, healing breaths of fresh air in whatever we do with adults. The book is *not* meant to be a compilation of teaching tips or teaching methods. It is, rather, a kind of charter for adult ministry or theology of adult ministry. It will address some of the struggles we face in getting adults together in these busy days to talk about God and ultimate questions. I do believe, however, that it could provide some guidance for pastors of adults, teachers and workers with adults, writers of curriculum, and anyone else who is interested in ministering to adults as we move together toward the 21st century.

This book will attempt to:

1. Survey the demographics and predictions for the 21st century

2. Point to some cultural and social obstacles to Christian education that are beginning to emerge

3. Consider the theological and biblical descriptions of what adults and adult education are

4. Discuss what adults are needing and wanting, especially in their adult Sunday School classes

I hope to challenge my fellow believers—both laity and clergy—to get involved in shaping a wonderful and workable future for the Christian education of adults. The goal is to renew adult education and ministry through the church. John Gardner reminds us that "no society is likely to renew itself unless its dominant orientation is to the future."[6]

I agree with George Roche when he writes: "We ourselves do not wish to predict the future, but to change it. For this we must understand the present by identifying its dominant ideas and the salesmen and preachers of these ideas."[7]

Let's learn from the past, and let's be aware of the challenges of the present. But let's walk into the future together to shape and renew our ministry with adults.

1

A World of Adults

Every nation is at a different stage of development. The scientific and technological countries grapple with problems different from those of emerging nations. Much of the data in the following section is from the U.S. Census Bureau and from researchers and futurists in the United States.

It is increasingly true, however, that we are rapidly becoming a global village. High-tech communication networks keep us in touch with what is happening throughout the world. How different from the world of 1865, where it took 12 days for London to learn that Abraham Lincoln had been assassinated.[1] As an interrelated global village of 5 billion people, what is happening in one part of the globe usually has some impact on the other parts. The United States will serve, then, as a microcosm of much that is happening to a greater or lesser degree around the world. The focus of our attention will be these areas: culture, population, home, marriage, family, work, leisure, and religion.

Culture

For thousands of years, ours was a world dominated by agriculture. Land was the basis of economy, life, culture, family structure, and politics. Life centered around the village. The pace was slow. People tended to live in large houses with grandparents, aunts, uncles, and cousins all living under the same roof. They worked together. They produced most of their own necessities. They were tied to the soil—almost immobile. For the most part the family was self-sufficient. They used energy resources that were renewable. Nature could grow more trees. The wind that propelled their sailboats and the water that turned the paddle wheels on their paddleboats was not destroyed by use. Even work animals would reproduce. Toffler calls this long period of agricultural dominance "The First Wave."

About 200 years ago (Toffler says 300 years ago) the industrial revolution swept across the world like a gigantic wave. Toffler writes, "An explosion was heard that sent concussive shock waves racing across the earth, demolishing ancient societies and creating a wholly new civilization."[2] This explosion was the industrial revolution. Where goods in the agricultural society were handcrafted, they now were mass-produced. Close-knit families and multigenerational households felt the stress of change. "As economic production shifted from the field to the factory, the family no longer worked together as a unit."[3] The family was often torn apart as people migrated from the farm to the city. The family was stripped of most relatives, and it grew smaller and more mobile. A new kind of family emerged—the nuclear family. It consisted of a father, mother, and a few children—but no encumbering relatives. Education of the children had been done in the home. Now education was turned over to the schools, and mass education emerged. The sick were now placed in hospitals. The elderly were placed in poorhouses, old-age homes, or nursing homes. Self-sufficiency was gone, and most people became dependent on what food, goods, and services others could produce.

"Nine to five" has become a phrase everybody understands. Although some worked shift work and some worked excessively long hours, this "eight to four" or "nine to five" marked off the workdays for millions of workers. Punctuality, which was not a particularly crucial issue in the early agricultural society, became a virtue in this new age of industrialism. People wore watches. If one group of workers was late getting their job done, others down the line were affected. It became a synchronized and clock-driven society. Great corporations and labor unions arose, bringing bureaucracy with them and wielding immense power.

"Industrialism broke society into thousands of interlocking parts," according to Toffler—"factories, churches, schools, trade unions, prisons, hospitals and the like. It broke the line of command between church, state, and individual. It broke knowledge into specialized disciplines. It broke jobs into fragments. It broke families into smaller units. In so doing, it shattered community life and culture."[4] One of the results of the industrial era has been the exploitation of irreplaceable fossil fuels like coal, gas, and oil.

Despite all the stress and changes and problems of the industrial era, the new technology has mass-produced incredible numbers of goods for distribution among the masses. Everything from shirts and shoes to automobiles and cameras and shampoo was produced. It has been an era of material abundance for large numbers of people. Toffler calls this period of industrialism "The Second Wave."

Two hundred years is not a very long lifespan for something as extensive as industrialism. But voices everywhere are sounding the death knell of industrialism and the rise of a new civilization. Toffler calls it "The Third Wave." Second-wave systems are in crisis. No more cheap energy. No more cheap raw materials. A new day is dawning. "A powerful tide is surging across much of the world today, creating a new, often bizarre, environment in which to work, play, marry, raise children, or retire."[5] The family is in crisis. The economy is reeling. Time-tested values are being questioned. Great industries are stumbling. Violent changes are occurring all around us. This is the case in the developed nations especially. (Many emerging third world nations are experiencing an industrialism much like we experienced 200 years ago.)

Patricia Cross believes that this new age into which we are moving will value knowledge and information above all else. She believes our society is increasingly dependent on knowledge. "Know-how and ideas have replaced land and machines as the economic assets of our society. Where we once talked about the agrarian society and then the industrial society, we now talk about the learning society."[6]

What will this "third wave society" do to the church? How will the so-called information society impact the way we train adults to become mature Christian believers in the future? Whatever its effect, we must not put our heads in the sand and deceive ourselves into believing that the world is forever the same. It is not the same. It will never be what it once was. And we must adapt. Better yet, we must help to innovatively shape the new day.

Toffler's conclusion is this:

> It is this third wave of change that will frame the rest of our lives. If we are to smooth the transition between the old dying civilization and the new one that is taking form, if we are to maintain a sense of self and the ability to manage our own lives through the intensifying crises that lie ahead, we must be able to recognize—and create—third wave innovations.[7]

And "third wave innovations" may be the key to an effective ministry with adults in the years ahead.

Population

World population grew from 1 billion in 1850 to 2 billion in 1930. It doubled in less than a century. In the mid-1950s, it stood at 2.75 billion, and today it stands at over 4.5 billion.[8] (The latest word is that it has passed 5 billion.) The total population in the United States is projected to increase from 230 million in 1980 to 268 million in the year 2000 and will reach an all-time high of 309 million in 2050.[9] Population increases are projected to be even greater in other world areas. John Stott observes that

> in a world that has become an interrelated global village of 4.5 billion men, women and children, the problems of human existence have reached crisis proportions. Modern man stretches to achieve new heights, but his very advances in technological and scientific realms threaten him with the loss of life's most precious gifts—and even life itself.[10]

The population of the United States is predicted to grow substantially older in the 21st century. The median age is projected to increase from 30.3 years in 1981 to 36.3 years in 2000 and 41.6 in 2050. (Median age means half the population is above and half below this age.) "Between now [1986] and the year 2000, nearly 21 million more men and women will be added to the escalating adult population."[11]

Life expectancy in the 18th century was in the early 40s. In 1900 life expectancy had risen to 47 years. The following chart will show how drastically it has risen recently and how it is projected to rise in the 21st century:[12]

Life-Expectancy Chart

	1981	*2005*	*2050*
Females	78.3	81.3	83.6
Males	70.7	73.3	75.1

Thousands of people are living to be centenarians (100 or

more years). Some predict there will be in excess of 100,000 centenarians in the United States (to say nothing of other world areas) by the year 2000.

Somebody once asked, "Who would want to live to be 90 years old?" The answer was: "The person who is 89." Assuming the person had good health, that is the obvious answer.[13]

For 30 years or more the young have ruled American life. For the next 20 years the middle aged will wield power. Around 2010 the old will begin to dominate. These predictions grow out of Cheryl Russell's demographical studies of the "baby-boom generation."[14] The first baby boomers (people born between 1946 and 1964) turned 40 on January 1, 1986. What that means is that the massive bulge in population known as the baby boom will move into middle age with as much gusto as they have moved through youth and young adult years. Seventy-six million people were born during this 19-year span called the baby boom. The baby boomers represent one-third of the total American population. Interestingly, Russell predicts that the middle aging of baby boomers will affect America in these significant ways:

1. It will make us more conservative.
2. It will make the home the focus of American life.
3. It will make the nation richer.[15]

The middle aging of America will not last forever. It will thrive until about 2010. Beginning around 2010, another dramatic transformation will take place. "When the baby boom retires, the old will dominate the country."[16] The percentage of the population aged 65 and over will rise from 11.4 percent in 1981 to 13.1 percent in 2000 to 21.7 percent in 2050. The 85 and over population will rise from 1.0 percent in 1981 to 1.9 percent in 2000 to 5.2 percent in 2050.[17] From 1975 to 1985, the adult population outgrew the general population by 4 million people.[18]

Among other things, population projections and estimates tell us that the focus of Christian ministry at the end of the 1900s and into the 21st century must be upon the adult.[19] There is no way around it. Either we will or we won't. It is a tough assignment because of the changing value systems and breakdown of marriage, home, and family. But, as it has demonstrated so many times in the past, the Church can rise to the challenge and create programs and structures and curriculum to meet the deep and unchanging needs of adults. "But anybody who thinks we can operate the same traditional ways we did a hundred years ago (would you believe twenty-five?) is not only shortsighted, he is blind," says Charles Swindoll. "The church of the 1980s and 1990s must get beyond the 1950s. The secret, of course, is adapting to our times without altering God's truth."[20]

Home

One of the most intriguing changes predicted involves the home. Many feel we are about to revolutionize what happens in our homes. Home was the center of life in the agricultural society, but it became little more than a place to sleep for many in the industrial age. The prediction is that the "third wave revolution" will draw the family back home. Toffler suggests that the home may very well become the center of society. It may become "the electronic cottage" where husbands, wives, and even children will *work* together as a unit.[21] Russell agrees that people will likely spend more time at home in the 21st century. She writes:

> The home will symbolize the social stability of the next few decades. It will be the center of American life, equipped with VCRs, home computers, compact disk stereo systems, cable television, large-screen and pocket-sized televisions, security systems, answering machines, microwaves, exercise equipment and a host of new technologies not yet on the drawing boards.[22]

There are predictions that people will order clothes to be delivered to the home. (Land's End clothes are already familiar to many.) Restaurants and grocery stores will deliver. A health club or exercise room will be set up in the home. Russell believes that "the home will be the focal point of entertainment in the 1990s because technological change is strengthening its role in people's lives."[23] The videocassette recorder has begun to make the home the center for adult socializing. "The VCR is bringing the baby boom back home," writes Russell.[24]

The "second wave" or industrial society was involved to a great degree in assembly-line work and the operation of giant manufacturing plants. It necessitated working outside the home in spacious manufacturing plants equipped with massive machines and run by skilled workers. Much of this skilled labor is being replaced today by robotics and other computerized machines. More and more, the workers are moving into "information handling" jobs. And many of these "information processing" jobs could be done at home. Many industries like Western Electric and Hewlett Packard are admitting that a high percentage of their work force could do most (if not all) of their work at home if they chose to go that direction. The following lines of work are already doing an incredible amount of work at home: salesmen, architects, designers, therapists, psychologists, music teachers, language instructors, art dealers, insurance agents, lawyers, academic researchers, and many more.[25]

Just equip a "work center" in your home with a computer, a printer, a copier, and a telephone, and the possibilities for homework are incredible. Such high-tech electronic equipment has precipitated the use of the term noted earlier, *electronic cottage*, to refer to the home of the 21st century. Certainly not everybody can or will want to work in the home, but there will probably be no good reason for 100 percent of the work force to be in the workshop or plant.

The predicted move back home will have many implications for the work of the Church. If the Church will respond by creating ways to use the home again as a place of Christian training and family worship, the return home could become a springboard for spiritual renewal. If, on the other hand, the return home causes people to become turned inward and unsociable and unwilling to meet together for adult Sunday School and corporate worship, then the Church will face real problems.

Marriage

A century ago, marriage was an economic necessity on the farm. It took the labor of both men and women to run the farm. It was not as economically critical during industrialism. The modern baby boomers are often two-income families and are finding marriage an economic necessity again.

In fact, predictions are that marriage will enjoy a resurgence, and divorce may even decline. The motivation for marriage, however, may be economic survival rather than other reasons. "The married and remarried will be comfortable —with money to spare," while the "single and divorced will find it hard to make ends meet." A marriage certificate will be a door to affluence. "Marriage is more important to a person's wallet than education, job skills or attitude toward work."[26] Could it be that in the 21st century a man would look for the wife who can best help him in the "electronic cottage"? Toffler suggests the following lyrics for a 21st-century love song:

> *I love your eyes, your cherry lips,*
> *The love that always lingers.*
> *Your way with words and random blips,*
> *Your skilled computer fingers.*[27]

Family

The fracture of the modern family is blamed on a variety

of factors like changing values, rock music, materialism, self-ishness, working mothers, and absentee fathers. Another factor in this obvious fragmentation is what Toffler calls the "general crisis of industrialism." He believes the pressures of a society totally sold out to industrialism is a major cause of family breakdown.

The "extended family" was the most common family model in the "first wave society" of agriculture. It brought several generations together under one roof. There were also "expanded families," which included unrelated orphans, farmhands, and boarders. (I was intrigued recently, while reading some material on my family tree, to notice that a number of my ancestors listed "boarders" at their residences on the 1850 census.)

The "nuclear family" has been prominent during industrialism but is not as prominent today. It consisted of a working husband, a houseworking wife, and two children. Evidence of the drastic breakdown of the nuclear family are the facts that only 7 percent of the total American population fits this description. Ninety-three percent no longer fit this nuclear family model primarily because of "working wives."[28]

The "work-at-home family" of the 21st century might be a return (in part) to the expanded family by inviting coworkers to join it.[29] Authorities disagree on whether the extended family or the nuclear family was most healthy.

The size of American families has been shrinking for years. They have shrunk from an average of 7 children in 1800 to 2 children in the 1930s to 1.8 children in the present.[30] Many couples in America, Europe, China, and the Soviet Union are choosing a "child-free" life-style. No children! They prefer "adult-centered homes."

Working mothers are another force to be reckoned with in the description of the modern family. In 1960, 50 percent of

American women were housewives. Currently only 20 percent are housewives. Russell described this phenomenon:

> The disappearance of the institution of the housewife has been so rapid and profound that many American businesses, churches and volunteer organizations have been caught between statistics and instincts. Most Americans were raised by full-time housewives. This is what makes the image of the housewife so powerful, though she is nearly extinct.[31]

More than half of American women work, and the prediction is that 80 percent will be working by 1995. Now that women have gained a place in the work world, they don't want to relinquish that place. Many would like to spend more time with their children, but they believe their families cannot afford it.

Another factor affecting the modern family is the skyrocketing of divorce. In 1962 there were 400,000 divorces recorded. About 20 years later, in 1981, this number had grown to 1.2 million. This means that millions of Americans (mostly women) are raising children alone, and most are struggling desperately to make ends meet. "59% of the baby boom's children will live with only one parent for at least a year before reaching age 18. 35% will live with a stepparent during part of their childhood."[32] A staggering 1 of every 7 American children is raised by a single parent. In Britain, nearly 1 family in 10 is headed by a single parent. In Germany, a special block of apartments are provided for such one-parent families including day child-care. These one-parent households are being called "the fastest-growing group in poverty."[33] "Solos" or people who live alone outside a family altogether have grown from 1.5 million in 1970 to 4.3 million in 1978.[34] "Singles by choice" have emerged as another significant force in society.

One of the greatest challenges (if not *the* greatest) for the 21st-century Church will be marriage and the family. What can we do to provide healing for sick families? What will it take to prevent further deterioration of home and family? How can we best minister to the divorced, to the children of divorce, to stepfamilies, and to the singles by choice?

Work

A normal greeting in our culture is "How do you do?" The real question that interests us, however, is "What do you do?"[35] Our work is important to us, and the work that others do captivates our interest. Pope John Paul II believed that "work is one of the characteristics that distinguishes man from the rest of creatures."[36] The world of work is changing. Jobs that once required a high school diploma now require a college degree. Some areas of work change so rapidly and drastically that workers are required to periodically retool and retrain just to keep up in their field. "The year 2000," some believe, "will mark the end of what has been called the American century."[37] The focus of work in the United States will change from a focus on manufacturing to the service industries. The location, hours, and structure of work will change. Work will likely be decentralized to where and when the customer wants it. The labor force will be smaller, and the average workweek will become shorter. The average age of the work force will be older. It is predicted that almost two-thirds of the new entrants into the work force between now and the year 2000 will be women. The view of work's meaning is also changing. Russell claims that there is a whole "new attitude among people in their 30s and 40s called 'backing off workaholism'! This means less demanding jobs, more flexible work schedules in order to have more time for relationships and personal interests."[38] The modern college kids, with whom I am privileged to work, are beginning to reflect this attitude. Many of them view "leisure" and exotic "trips" and "time off" as a necessity rather than a luxury. They do not view these as something that must be earned through hard work. They view them as rights. "A generation of Americans," says Cheryl Russell, "has come to see leisure as a birthright."[39]

Leisure

Despite the fact that we expect and demand more leisure, that leisure is often filled up with other things or is used in a most unleisurely way. A Louis Harris survey shows that the average American has 18 hours of leisure each week, 8 hours less than 10 years ago. Travel is becoming a significant and growing leisure expenditure. Several long-weekend vacations through the year seem to be preferable to a single two- or three-week vacation. Quick foreign trips, short cruises, and weekend jaunts seem to be the wave of the future. *"The baby boom hungers after and is willing to pay for experiences."*[40] I think the preceding statement is the most impressive and revealing statement in Cheryl Russell's book. It describes precisely how many today (both inside and outside the Church) really feel. It raises the question, "Is it a part of the role of the Church to provide such experiences?"

Religion

Not many years ago there were dire predictions about the future of religion. We were told we were entering a post-Christian era. The feeling was that religious institutions and traditions were in irreversible decline. Even the death of God was proclaimed.[41]

The opposite is proving to be true. Instead of the decline or death of religion, "we are witnessing a resurgence of tradi-tional religion in the world."[42] Even in the Soviet Union and China, religion seems to be assuming a more public role. Recently the Soviet Union celebrated the 1,000th year of Chris-tianity in the country. General Secretary Gorbachev met with leaders of the Russian Orthodox church. It was the first meeting of this kind by a party secretary since 1943. Mrs. Gorbachev visited the great Christian celebration that was held in the famous Bolshoi Theater. The evening television newscasts featured the conference highlights. One older woman who had come from Leningrad to Moscow stated: "I'm no longer afraid to tell people I'm a Christian," as tears streamed down her cheeks.[43]

"More than 4,000 Protestant churches and tens of thousands of home worship meetings are now functioning in China," according to *Christianity Today* magazine. The Red Guard closed and ransacked churches, beat and humiliated believers, and burned Bibles during the Cultural Revolution. Despite great suffering, Christians have visibly bloomed since churches were reopened in 1979. Religious freedom is still fragile, but a new generation of leaders is emerging to guide their growing flocks. "That makes their elders, who held onto faith in the darkest days, very happy."[44]

The return to religion in America, however, is *not* totally a return to traditional religion. There *is* a resurgence of the Christian evangelical movement, which has used television, radio, and Christian books to fuel the so-called born-again movement. This movement has already had a significant impact in the political arena. This return to religion has also included about every kind of bizarre religious belief imaginable. Combinations of nature worship, Eastern mysticism, existential philosophy, human potential psychology, cults, and occultic groups have emerged. Each little group has its own "scientific priesthood or 10-minute guru." Some have even claimed the ability to channel the teachings of 25,000-year-old ancestors. Without a doubt, "colliding visions rock our mental universe."[45] A recent poll conducted by the Williamsburg Charter Foundation, a nonprofit, nonsectarian group, found that most Americans want more government control of cults and believe the worship of Satan should be illegal. The same poll found that *one* out of *five* secularists believe that evangelicals have too much power and influence. *One* out of every *three* in the academic community thought that evangelicals are a threat to democracy.[46]

Christianity continues to be the largest religious community in the United States. Jews have been the second-largest religious group but are about to be surpassed by the rapidly growing Islamic religion. Muslims now represent 14 percent of the immigrants coming to America. Couple that with their high birthrate, and they are expected to surpass the Jews in number in less than 30 years. There are an estimated 4.6 million U.S. Muslims. Many Muslims stay because of the freedom of expression to practice Islam in the true sense. Others return to their homelands as leaders.[47]

The resurgence of religion in our world is a wonderful open door of opportunity for us. Among others things, it indicates an openness to the basic religious quest of the human heart. The 21st century could be the time when the kingdom of God could come into many millions of lives in China and the Soviet Union as well as around the world.

On the other hand, with the emergence of the New Age movement and all the other pseudoreligions and cults, the Christian Church will need to be at its very best spiritually and intellectually to meet the challenge. What a convincing argument for a strong, relevant, and biblically-theologically sound program of Christian adult education in the Church!

Having looked at some of the research and predictions of several notable authors, it would seem that the Church will need to give attention to and create structures or programs to address such 21st-century topics as the following:

1. The global village
2. The information society
3. The aging population
4. The return home

5. The economic necessity of marriage
6. The clash over gender roles
7. The role of singles by choice
8. The new work ethic
9. The hunger for leisure in the Christian's life
10. The challenge of new religions

With these topics as a guide for our planning, we have the opportunity to build a program of Christian adult education and ministry that will address the real issues with which adults are grappling. If we don't fumble the ball, and if we find the mind of the Lord in our planning, we could turn the corner with adults and make a significant impact on the early part of the 21st century. If we are unable to make the turn, the Church will lose, and the world will suffer from it.

With this futuristic data in our minds, let's turn in the next chapter to a discussion of some of the hindrances to Christian education. You will notice that many of the so-called obstacles are direct outgrowths of the rapidly changing society in which we live. Others are symptoms of our moral and spiritual breakdown.

2

Obstacles to Christian Education

The Christian Church has always lived in a changing world. Every generation has faced new challenges. It is true that the Church has not always been willing to change. When it *has* changed, it has been slow to do it. And not all of its changes have been good ones.

Probably the most critical changes of the Church have been the subtle and gradual ones. The culture around us has quietly and unobtrusively become a part of us. This is especially true in the 20th century. Almost without realizing exactly what was happening, we became different; we were changed. We had not planned to change, nor did we wake up one morning intending to change. But it became obvious to us that somewhere along the way we did change, and we were different from before.

Some of the changes we have made have not been particularly detrimental to the Christian education program of the Church. Instead, they have been stimulating and helpful. There are, however, other changes that have happened or are happening that are cause for great concern because they are hindrances to the Church's educational thrust. The following are proving to be obstacles to Christian education as we move into the 21st century.

Overstimulated Senses

There is nothing inherently wrong with having our senses stimulated. God created us as sensory creatures and apparently expected us to enjoy seeing, hearing, smelling, tasting, and touching. He created so many wonderful things to bring us pleasure while we live in this world. The writer of Ecclesiastes was beginning to understand the place of pleasure when he said: "A man can do nothing better than to eat and drink and find satisfaction in his work" (Eccles. 2:24). In fact, he withheld no pleasure from his heart. His conclusion was, however, that the pursuit of pleasure did *not* bring ultimate meaning to his life. An overcommitment to pleasure left him feeling that life was meaningless and was like chasing the wind.

Many contemporary Christians have become oversaturated by television watching, video viewing, and stereo listening. Some have spent years listening to loud stereo music on a Sony Walkman and watching stimulating music videos. Their emotions have been torn by violent and sexually stimulating shows on television. Increasingly they are becoming so sensually stimulated that they are turned off by anything that does not give them another "high." The result is boredom or a feeling of boredom. This has become the byword of this generation: *boring.* A girl at college had a personalized license plate on her red sports car that gives her philosophy of life: BORING. Arnold Toynbee speaks to this tendency to boredom in his book *Surviving the Future* when he says, "Human beings, for the most part, quickly become bored with idleness, and sooner or later, I think, they also become sated with watching sports and even taking part in it."[1]

The world is captivated by the electronic media—especially television. There is a "global fascination with watching picture tubes."[2] It has been said: "If you don't watch television more than four hours a day, you're in the culture but not of it."[3]

Charles Colson believes TV is the single most powerful medium of communication. Recent studies show that the TV set is turned on in U.S. homes an average of seven hours each day. While some of it is quality programming, and it is surely not all bad, "Much of it," writes Colson, "simply promotes moral decay."[4] Why is there such a global fascination with the television set? How could it hold so many people in its grip? George Roche addresses this very issue in his book *A World Without Heroes.*

> The mighty mechanism we have erected to glut our senses and escape our unhappiness is a marvel to rival our science and industry. . . . of our presumed 72 hours of leisure per week, we spend, on average, over 44 staring at the tube. Catering to every visual or tactile sensation, vicarious thrill and carnal urge, our culture promises happiness in every measure, for every purse, to every taste. We pursue it till we are weary, but can never hold it long, for in the end, there is no escape.[5]

The young adults of today are children of the television and video age. When they come to my college classroom, they bring with them the very things Roche has mentioned. They have logged so many hours of passively sitting in front of a television set and have been hyped by so many thousands of commercials that their senses are indeed glutted. They have vicariously witnessed so many shocking scenes and carry with them so many exotic images that they are easily bored by anything that is not a production or a song and dance. Lest I overkill the topic of television, let me readily admit that television is with us to stay. Esperanto is not the universal language, television is. In the United States, "scarcely any home is too poor, too rich, or too remote to have a television set. Everybody speaks the language of television."[6] This is increasingly true in the world at large. There are no indications of which I am aware to suggest that the influence of television and the media is decreasing. Whatever the case, we need to find ways to counteract the grip that television is holding over many of our people today.

These young adults whose senses have been overstimulated will be the middle and senior adults of the 21st century. It is they who will make Christian adult education come alive or let it slip quietly away. I am finding that many of them are "fed up to here" with such a passive and vicarious way of living. They are *open to* and *ready to* make contact with real-life situations and issues. They are hungry to do something to meet a real need or solve a real problem. Our challenge will be to lead them out of the four walls of the church or home into the arena of real ministry to meet human needs.

Entertainment Inertia

This is the result of the first obstacle, "overstimulated senses." Because of such an oversaturation in entertainment of all forms, we have become a society of spectators.

We are entertained because we want to be entertained. It is *not* something that is forced on us. We do have a choice. Most of us choose to be entertained. Individuals and families have to fight against the prevailing currents to avoid sitting, watching, listening, spectating, and vegetating. Chuck Swindoll believes this driving desire to be entertained and amused is due to our lack of mental self-control. His criticism is a stinging one. "The overindulgence and underachievement of our age," he writes, "have created a monster whose brain is lazy, vision is blurred, hands are greedy, skin is thin, middle is round, and seat is wide. Color him baby blue."[7]

So prevalent is this condition, a new term has been coined to describe those persons under the grip of "entertainment inertia." They are being called "couch potatoes." This term is meant to depict those who habitually sit on the couch like zombies and watch endless hours of television and videos.

We have become a big-event culture. There is something about being part of a gigantic crowd of people in a stadium or being part of a big event in a large church. We like to come together and be entertained. We also like to applaud somebody or something. We have become the applause culture. We are so highly trained that we know when to clap, when *not* to clap, and when to stand and clap. You know you are a big hit when you receive a standing ovation. Though I hear some fine people criticize clapping in church, I must admit that it doesn't bother me that much. In light of the fact that "Hallelujahs" and "Praise the Lords" and "Glory to Gods" seem to have died out or have been squelched, it seems appropriate to me that we should at least clap our praises to the great God of the universe once in a while. Otherwise, the stones are going to cry out (Luke 19:40).

Another avenue of modern entertainment is the exotic trip. Everything from weekend jaunts to Caribbean cruises has become a modern form of entertainment. Next year we have to outdo what we did this year. Even restaurants cater to having "an eating experience" with special decor, music, and specially trained waiters. They refer to it as "ambience."

Such overstimulated and entertainment-numbed people are not very good candidates for a 9:30 A.M. Sunday School class or a 7 P.M. Wednesday night prayer meeting. It is not always a total lack of interest. It may simply be a matter of inertia, boredom, or sheer physical or emotional fatigue.

This inertia carries over in our attitudes to worship. "Too often we sit in church as spectators," claims Charles Colson, "waiting for the needy multitudes to come watch the show with us. But for those in need—spiritually and physically—a fat, lethargic church preoccupied with its own entertainment holds no appeal."[8]

Part of our problem is that we (the Church) have become so comfortable with the culture that we are almost blinded to its egocentric and materialistic ways. Many of us are like passengers sailing along in a great ship, mesmerized by music and lights, while the ship drifts aimlessly along or is steered into catastrophe.[9] We seem to be mute and powerless to do anything about it. Some have so bought into the culture that their decisions seem to be made by television programs, their values created by television directors, and their biases are those of the television networks.

What an opportunity for the Church to intervene! We can gently and lovingly lead the people from the fantasy and plastic world of entertainment, where nothing is nailed down and everything goes, to the world of the Word of God, where there is something on which you can build your life.

Decreased Feeling of Need for Others

People who work with adults can attest to the truth of this claim. People do not seem to need to get together today in the same ways they did in the past. Many people of *all age-groups* today are more interested in a "quiet night at home" than a busy night of fellowship at the church.

In agrarian times, the church and Sunday School were places where primary social needs were met. This is not necessarily true today. For one thing, most people who work in our culture work with people. Some work with great numbers of different people. Some fly all over the world to work with people. This is a far cry from the little self-contained farm communities where extended families once resided.

Our tendency today is to look for reasons *not* to get together with others. This is unfortunate, but it is true of many in the Church and in the world today.

Another factor is the increased feeling of independence of our culture and feelings of self-sufficiency. When we can work at home and be entertained at home, and sleep and eat at home, there is little feeling of need to go elsewhere.

Not only is this stay-at-home tendency true of adults, but also it is becoming increasingly true of youth and children. Given a choice of either going to Sunday School (or some other group) or staying home and watching a video, many would choose to stay home and engage in vicarious experiences.

I will discuss this phenomenon later, but the vicarious has taken the place of the actual or real in the lives of many people.

The tragedy of this self-sufficient attitude is that we cut ourselves off from terribly needy persons to whom we could minister. They need our ministry, and we need to minister. Otherwise we turn inward and try to live off of ourselves; and before we know it, we are spiritually dead. My pastor recently told an intriguing story about the great Belgian draft horses. One of these magnificent horses is so strong that it is able to pull *1 ton* by itself. That's quite a feat. More incredible, though, is the fact that when two horses are harnessed together, they are said to be able to pull *16 tons!* What a difference it makes when we pull together! This a good reason to be a part of a loving Sunday School class or local church.

Decreased Feeling of Need for the God Concept

There is a strong undercurrent of belief in society that mankind can do anything he sets his mind to do. These people will admit that there was a time when "primitive man" did not understand the mysteries of life. He needed the "God concept" to explain life's mysteries. But in our modern scientific and technological age, most all our questions are answered. I mean, we can send man around the moon, transplant human organs, and engineer the genetic structure of new human life. What else do we need?

The God concept worked fine before man had created so much and understood so much, but the God concept is archaic and out-of-date today. Man has matured; man has come of age. We no longer need such superstition. Everything we are and everything we need is in the natural and biological realm. There is really no such thing as a supernatural realm. Few moderns are really leaning on or depending on the so-called God idea. Protagoras stated it millennia ago, "Man is the measure of all things." The New Age movement is picking up the chant today.

Eve, in the Garden of Eden, was the first to express the feeling that God might not be necessary. Her temptation was not really a piece of fruit. The real temptation was the offer *to be like God.* The tempter enticed her by saying, "God knows that when you eat of it your eyes will be opened, and you will be like God" (Gen. 3:5). She would be like God? This fed her pride and stimulated her appetite for self-worship. Toynbee agrees that self-worship is the paramount religion of mankind, although it appears in many different ways.[10]

In a sense, the modern world has made an "insane inversion of the Garden of Eden." In Eden, God expelled Adam and Eve for trying to become divine. In our modern world, men and women are driving God out in order to create an earthly paradise.[11]

This search for God in the human self is a vain and fruitless search. The only true way to find meaning and purpose is in the surrender of self in obedience to Christ, and not in a search for self.[12]

No century in the history of the world will be in greater need of a sovereign God to guide them through the mazes of complex living than the 21st. We must believe, preach, teach, and embody the truth of an Almighty God who is at work in the world He created.

Crippling Effects of Fast-Lane Living

Most of us find ourselves operating in the "fast lanes" of

life—the fast lane of the workplace, the schoolroom, the market. Increasingly, even our homes are becoming freeways of fast living.

We may sleep in the same house but arise at different times, go different directions, return at different times, and even eat meals at different times. This describes exactly what our home was like when all the kids were home.

Some refer to it as "the rat race." This refers to our frenetic running to and fro and back again in quest of a crumb or two or a piece of cheese, frantically pursuing we know not what; and when we expend our available energy, we redouble our efforts and tear out again.

"Stress City" is what others call it. Most fast-lane people are tired, fatigued, washed out. When they come home at night, they really do not want to go anywhere else. They simply want to curl up in a chair or lie down on a couch and relax.

"Speed is considered one of the chief virtues in our society."[13] We are always in a rush. We detest waiting in lines. We are committed to movement and action and getting things done. We are aggressive, task-oriented, and success-motivated. A poem by D. Schwartz aptly describes this fast-lane life-style:

> *My heart beating, my heart running,*
> *The light brimming,*
> *My mind moving, the ground turning,*
> *My eyes blinking, the air flowing,*
> *The clock's quick ticking,*
> *Time moving, time dying,*
> *Time perpetually perishing.*[14]

I love to read the writings of Henry David Thoreau. He seemed to have discovered the simple pleasures that make life rewarding and meaningful. Although I do not accept some of his theological positions, he has some important things to say to fast-lane people:

I went to the woods because I wished to live deliberately, to front only the essential facts of life, and see if I could not learn what it had to teach, and not, when I came to die, discover that I had not lived. . . . I wanted to live deep and suck out all the marrow of life, to live so sturdily and Spartanlike as to put to rout all that was not life, to cut a broad swath and share close, to drive life into a corner, and reduce it to its lowest terms.[15]

Thoreau sums it all up in a memorable little statement: "Our life is frittered away by detail."[16] It is true, isn't it? Lives frittered away, nerves tattered, body damaged, and even the will to live broken down by such insane fast-lane living.

I believe that one of the secrets to the success of the adult Sunday School in the 21st century will be proportionate to how adequately we can create an "oasis" or "recreating rest stop" along the fast lanes of living for those who attend.

Broken Homes and Fractured Families

The breakdown of marriages and the destruction of the typical family is forcing us to rethink our whole approach to Christian education. We have to be careful and thoughtful, for example, about how we group people together. The last thing in the world we want to do in the church is to create another barrier or add to the heavy load of the divorced or children of divorce. To insist on "couples classes" immediately alienates the divorced.

We have to be careful what we say. To ask the children to "go home and discuss this question with your father" can be a source of strain and embarrassment to a child of divorce.

I have found it a real challenge to assimilate the divorced or widowed into a meaningful Sunday School arrangement. Many resist being isolated into a "singles class." They do not think of themselves as single yet. Some never do. Many prefer to become or remain a part of a couples class. A friend of mine lost his wife to cancer some time ago. He and his wife were greeters at the church. He has continued to greet by himself. I asked one day what was most difficult for him at church. His response was not what I expected. He said, "The most difficult thing I face on Sunday morning is walking into the sanctuary after I've finished greeting people and sitting down by myself. I just wish somebody would ask me to sit by them." I have a sneaking suspicion that much of the ministry that hurting people need involves such simple and easy-to-do things as saying, "Come and sit with me today," or "Let's have lunch together this Tuesday." The tragedy is, because we do not know what to say to the divorced and widowed, we don't say anything.

Many of these people who have been devastated by divorce or the loss of a mate really need a counseling approach to Christian education, more than an informational approach. They need a kind of therapy more than they need facts or a lecture. A pastor recently told me about the young adult class he has been teaching in his local church. The class had seemed to stagnate and was really not growing or alive. Something happened, however, that shook the class to its senses: A couple in the class divorced. The woman left; the man remained in the class. Immediately the class began to minister to this hurting man. Sunday after Sunday, whatever the scripture may have been, they always seemed to be able to find ways to apply it to this victim of divorce. The pastor said, "It literally transformed the class. They rallied around him and ministered to him, and it ignited a fire. The class has started to grow again." Some of the most successful adult classes are informal, open, creating, releasing, healing, need-meeting times.

I am convinced that we do not have the luxury of making the adult Sunday School hour a time for highly technical or deeply complex or higher-critical studies. (These are important, but not for Sunday School.) The primary task of the teacher of adults, it seems to me, is to prayerfully find ways to understand the implications of the scripture and to push them up against the needs and hurts of the class member.

Bishop Wilke tells us what hurting people want and need: "Today people are confused and lonely, overstimulated and bewildered. . . . They want a familiar friend, a pastor they know, and a spiritual leader who can take them spiritually deeper than they have ever gone before."[17]

There is reason to believe that broken homes and fractured families will also be a problem that will need to be addressed by the 21st century.

The Pressure of Materialism

The urge to get has never been greater. We have literally become a consumer culture. If you were to pose the question, "What is man?" television would have a ready answer: "Men and women are consumers."[18] Our media age seems to look on everything as a product. Everything has a price and is meant to be consumed. One of the incredible problems with all this is the fact that "a non-Christian view of life predominates the news media, as it does in society."[19] What the media and society promote are not necessarily what Christians want or need.

A big problem among many Christians today is that they do not seem to discern the false values of our culture. We have tended to accept whatever our culture tells us is good and right. "Tragically, the church has become so comfortable with the culture," writes Charles Colson, "it can no longer see the bankruptcy of its egocentric, materialistic ways."[20]

It is so convenient to be a consumer today. In most American cities, there are convenience stores in every neighborhood. It is even possible today to order fast food or clothes or groceries over the telephone. It is so convenient to buy "stuff." Once it was radios, then television. Now it's videocassette recorders and compact disc players. I wonder what will be next?

Materialism is not a disease just of the affluent. It impacts the whole of society. I remember years ago noticing how many old, run-down shacks, with a car or two out front on blocks, would also have a television antenna on top of the house. I always wondered how such obviously poor people could afford such. Recently I was struck with a new phenomenon. These same little run-down shacks are there. Many of the same people live there, but now there is a satellite dish out in the yard.

To be honest about it, there is nothing especially wrong with getting or consuming. Unless we get and consume, we die. The pressure comes, however, when we take on extra jobs, work much longer hours, spend less time at home with wife/husband and children, and are forced to absent ourselves from the work of God and the church. If we are not careful, a greedy drive to get and consume will grip us; and we will injure our family relationships, strain our marital relationship, and even destroy our physical health. There is *no hint whatsoever* that the pressure of materialism will subside in future days.

Here is the danger of materialism as described by the Old Testament prophet Hosea: "With their silver and gold they made idols for their own destruction" (Hos. 8:4, RSV). Idols can become such an integral part of our society and culture that, after a time, they are difficult to identify. The people of Jerusalem became so accustomed to the worship of Molech in the Temple that they began to view it as normal. It seemed *odd* to them that the prophets would come in and denounce the practice.[21] This creeping acceptance of our surrounding cultural beliefs and values is so subtle but so devastating to the life of the church.

Adults of every generation need to know what the Bible has to say about money and worldly goods and things. This can become a most profitable area for study and discussion in an adult Sunday School class.

The Pressure of Time

What creates "time pressures"? There is apparently the same amount of time in a modern day as in an ancient day. The majority of people I know, however, use expressions like this: "I don't have enough time. I'm running out of time. I am going to have to work overtime. There are not enough hours in the day." What's the problem with time? Somebody suggested that "time" was no problem until somebody invented the watch. Once we could measure time so precisely, time began to pressure us. The first clock apparently had only an hour hand; but the industrial revolution (Toffler's second wave) and the railroad train demanded more precise time units, so the minute hand was added. With the coming of the space age, we have added the second hand and have broken time down further into milliseconds and microseconds.

Maybe we have made life too complex. Maybe we are trying to pack too much into the available time units of the day. Whatever is happening, many people view time as something akin to the devil. They are constantly under terrible time pressure, always late, huffing and puffing, and moaning and groaning about time. They are forever looking forward to the day when, as they describe it, "I will have more time!" But that day never comes. The result is stress, fatigue, depression, and even panic at times. One of my class members recently told me, "The reason I do not come to your Sunday School class anymore is that those few moments on Sunday morning are the only time during the whole week that my wife and I can have breakfast together and talk." Both work excessively long hours.

Hans Kung says, "People are going round in circles in the cage of their planet, because they have forgotten that they can look up to the sky—because all we want is to live, it has become impossible for us to live."[22]

A well-planned Sunday School class can provide a few moments on Sunday mornings for adults to get off the treadmill and out of their "cages." It can offer them a few moments of solace and a breath of fresh air. When Leonardo da Vinci was painting his *Last Supper,* he was chided for standing hours before the canvas without making a stroke. He explained, "When I pause the longest, I make the most telling strokes with my brush."[23] There is probably nothing that 21st-century adults will need more than moments for pause and reflection before they return to the world to make their marks.

Changing Concepts of Reality

Underlying many of our contemporary struggles is the matter of an inordinate concern for the present. For many modern pagans, God is dead, and there is no past and no future. All we have is the "present, existential moment," the "now"! They have no interest in studying lessons from the past or strategies for the future. The only reality that exists is the "now," and I personally create my own *reality,* my own *truth,* and my own *values* by the choices I make.

The prevailing attitude, then, is "Capture the moment." Enhance it. Expand it. Live in the now. Savor the moments. Grab all the gusto you can today. You'd better get it now, because this is all there is. There is no such thing as a supernatural, no such thing as life after death, no such person as God. You are "God." You will find all the meaning you are ever going to find in the present, physical realm. This is it!

Schlossberg criticized the Protestant church at this point. "Protestantism has largely divested itself of the transcendent," he claims, "and has become almost indistinguishable from the surrounding culture."[24] When you lose the transcendent, supernatural realm, you are forced to decide, then, what is reality and what is unreality in the present world. I have noticed recently that many television-age young people have a tendency to view what happens on television as *reality*. They discuss with animation and excitement some fictional program they have seen as if it *really* did happen, and they tend to treat actual, everyday, real-world happenings as if they were fantasy or unimportant. A subtle but serious inversion of reality is happening in our culture.

What a wonderful opportunity to discuss this critical philosophical question, "What is real?" The Christian faith distinguishes between those things that are "real" and those that are "ultimately real." Too many moderns have been absorbed in the pagan notion that this world and this present moment is all there is to life. We must never let the people forget that we are really "strangers and pilgrims" in this world. This world is not my final home. My destination is a heavenly home, "whose builder and maker is God" (Heb. 11:13, 10, KJV).

Apathy

"Apathy and lowered motivation are the most widely noted characteristics of a civilization in decline," writes John Gardner. "Apathetic men and women accomplish nothing. Those who believe in nothing change nothing for the better. They renew nothing and heal no one, least of all themselves."[25]

This is a kind of passive attitude that says, "I don't really care about any of this stuff." It is not necessarily a vicious opposition, but neither is it an excited acceptance. The most characteristic gesture of this modern apathetic individual is a shrug of the shoulders. The shrug speaks volumes.

Pastor Charles Stanley believes the "I don't care attitude" is the greatest problem the church faces. He quotes an unknown Christian's description of the attitude of apathy:

> When Gideon was through thinning out his frightened and indifferent soldiers, he discovered that only one out of one hundred was brave and really meant business. . . . The unorganized indifference within the ranks of the church

members is far more destructive to the work of the Lord than all the organized forces of inquiry assailing from the outside.[26]

There is good reason to believe that this apathy is the consequence or result of the various factors we have already discussed: overstimulation, entertainment, lack of fellowship, no need for God, fast-lane living, broken homes, pressures of materialism and time, and a changing idea of reality. It is an attitude of: "I'm overstimulated, overentertained, and overhyped all week long! I rush to work and back. I'm tired, washed out. I'll just stay home with my computer, my television, and my VCR. I can be taught, be preached at, and worship over television and save myself a bundle of stress!"

Apathy describes too many of us in the Christian Church who are either uninvolved and unconcerned or overcommitted and stressed out. Too many of us have tried to reform culture by embracing as much of it as we can. In the process, we have tended to become a "cultural church." The distinctive message of the Church has been diluted, and its mission or reason for existence has become unclear. I talked recently to an individual who had just attended a conference of leaders of a particular church. When he returned from the conference, he informed me that the leaders spent several days trying to decide what the mission of the Church really is. They were no longer sure why they existed.

What can we do about the encroachment of culture into the Church? How can we be a vital part of society without getting enamored with society's non-Christian values? How can we overcome these obstacles and make Christian adult education happen in the future?

There are three possible approaches to culture:

1. *Culture embracers.* Christians can embrace or buy into the culture around them, adopting the general characteristics of culture, and become absorbed in culture.

2. *Culture rejecters.* These people react against prevailing culture by rejecting its norms and resisting its changing patterns. They try to hold onto and conserve a simpler or "proven" way of life.

3. *Culture transformers.* They attempt neither to adopt nor reject the culture; rather, they try to move into existing culture and make it better and to restore it to what it should be.[27] This matter of "culture transformation" is what we are called to do as we become "salt" and "light" in the world (Matt. 5:13-16). A program of Christian adult education that fails to show its people how to be salt and light in the surrounding culture has no good reason to call itself Christian.

3

A Theology of Adults

The most meaningful questions in life are theological questions. Every generation, every century, and every millennium needs to answer them. In spite of an age of rapidly accelerating change and the accompanying obstacles and hindrances it presents to the Church, we must answer these critical questions. The basic needs and questions of mankind are essentially the same, whatever the century. Adults spend inordinate amounts of their time grappling with these questions. If the adult education program of the 21st-century Church is to be effective, it must help its adults find answers to these questions. Six of the most critical of these questions are the following:

1. From where did I come? (Beginnings)
2. Why am I here? (Meanings)
3. Who am I? (Relationships)
4. What should I do? (Callings)
5. What is important? (Truths)
6. Where am I going? (Directions)

"Theology, in the simplest terms, is our human attempt to think clearly and correctly about God." So state the writers of *God, Man, and Salvation* . It is also our attempt to know who we are and how we fit in the universe. This is precisely what most adults are trying to do when they address such questions as the six listed above. "No person, religious or otherwise, can escape the need to grapple with problems of the source and nature of reality and the meaning and destiny of life."[1]

I am discovering that there is an immense openness among contemporary adults (both inside and outside the Church) to discuss these critical questions of human existence. There is a special openness among "people in crisis." A most recent opportunity for me has been my neighbor. We have lived beside these people for 10 years. When we first moved in, Steve informed me he was not interested in discussing religion or being bothered. We have tried to be good neighbors but have been careful not to "bother" them. They have lived like so many in our secular society: buying, accumulating, eating, drinking, smoking, and making money.

Suddenly, about a year ago, things changed. Steve said, "Richard, I just returned from the doctor's office. I have massive, inoperable lung cancer." I expressed my concern and told him I would pray for him. He said, "Thanks, I really need it." Sitting out on his front porch a few days later, Steve said to me, "I guess you think I never have any thoughts about God, but I do. I want you to know, Richard, I do believe in God." A few months later, I sat beside his hospital bed and held his hand as we talked about life, death, God, and human destiny. He was gasping for air and was obviously near the end. Before I left, I knelt down close to his ear and prayed with him a prayer of forgiveness and asked the Lord to aid him in these moments. Thirty minutes after I left, he quietly died. We have had a continuing opportunity to minister to the wife and children. Much of our conversation has to do with these questions.

A Theology of Beginnings

This is an attempt to answer the question, "From where

did I come?" "Beginnings" is an important topic to all ages but especially to adults. Not only do some adults want to trace their family tree and discover their roots or beginnings, but they also want to know the origin of the universe and the source of human existence.

Some modern scientists believe that life began by chance chemical encounters in the rich primordial soup that once covered the earth. Out of this primordial soup, life developed into higher forms through genetic selection of characteristics that enhanced survival. This conglomeration finally produced the human species that will eventually pass into extinction.[2]

The message of the Bible is that "in the beginning God created the heavens and the earth" (Gen. 1:1). Then "God created man in his own image" (v. 27). Genesis 1—11 is a book of origins that deals with the origin of the universe, of life, of order on the earth, of mankind, of sin, of violence and disorder, and of nations and languages. If you want to read about beginnings or origins, read Genesis 1—11. In answer to the question, "Who made all things?" the Scripture boldly answers, "God created."

A Christian believer is not hesitant to say, "God is the Source of the universe and human life. He is the Beginning, the First Cause, the reason for my being!" The Christian would also point to *history*. The paramount Christian message about history is that the dividing line of history between B.C. and A.D. is the coming of Jesus Christ into history. When He came, He brought the spiritual and physical realms together. He brought eternity into time. Past, present, and future come together in Christ. Not only did He create life, but He is "the life" (John 1:3-4; 14:6).

The adult needs to develop his own "theology of beginnings." This commitment of belief will impact almost everything else one believes. My pastor recently told this delightful story about Britain's royal yacht. The captain was carrying

Prince Charles and Princess Diana, sailing along on the ocean at night. Suddenly the captain saw lights approaching. He sent an urgent signal, "Please alter course!" A message came back, "You alter course!" The angered captain replied, "This is John Jones, captain of the royal yacht. The Prince and Princess are on board. In the name of and by the authority of the Queen, *you change course!*" An answer came back, "This is Fred Smith, and I have been keeper of this lighthouse for 22 years, and *I can't change course.*"

A settled theology of beginnings can serve as a lighthouse for citizens of the 21st century. When everyone and everything around you is yelling, "Alter course!" it will hold you steady.

A Theology of Meanings

This is an attempt to answer the questions, "Why am I here? What is the meaning of life?" The quest for meaning is as ancient as Adam and Eve. The proposals for finding meaning are as contemporary as the morning newspaper. "Humans are in their nature seekers of meaning," says Gardner. "They cannot help being so any more than they can help breathing or maintaining a certain body temperature."[3] The quest for meaning should be a prominent topic in any healthy program for adult Christian education.

The contemporary secular answer to the quest for meaning involves working long hours, accumulating many things, looking out for yourself, and making your pleasure the driving force of your life. "Being busy," writes Henri Nouwen, "has become a status symbol."[4] Most of us encourage each other to keep the body and mind in constant motion. With these goals in mind, some expend all their energies in pursuit of one more pleasurable high, while others become workaholics and sell their very lives to the company store. In neither case do they find life's ultimate meaning. Alexander Solzhenitsyn cut to the heart of the quest for meaning with these unforgettable words from a Soviet prison: "The meaning of earthly existence is not, as we have grown used to thinking, in prosperity, but in the development of the soul."[5]

Our human tendency is to think, I could find meaning if I lived in that city or had that job or was married to that person. It is "the lie of the greener pasture." Finding meaning has to do with learning to accept who you are, where you are, and what you have. Thoreau mentions how he once longed to live in a different era or at a different place.

> We are wont to imagine rare and delectable places in some remote and more celestial corner of the system, behind the constellation Cassiopeia's Choir, far from noise and disturbance. I discovered that my house actually had its site in such a withdrawn, but forever new and unprofaned, part of the universe.[6]

The truth of the matter is that *you can find meaning* where you live, where you work, with whom you are, and with the one to whom you are married.

If success is not the key to meaning in life, then what is? Colson summed it up beautifully when he wrote, "God calls us, not to success, but to faith—obedience and trust and service—and He bids us to be unconcerned with measuring our work the way the world does. We are to sow; He will reap as He pleases."[7]

The baby boomers (who are now becoming middle adults) searched for freedom in the 1960s, for identity in the 1970s, for careers in the 1980s, and will no doubt search for meaning in the 2030s.[8] If there is anything the Christian Church should be prepared to dispense to a changing world, it is meaning. To share Christ is to dispense meaning. This will be as critically important in the 21st century as it ever was.

A Theology of Relationships

This is an attempt to answer the questions, "Who am I?

How do I relate to others?" A study of relationships must begin with an understanding of "Who am I?" Am I a person of inestimable value or am I expendable? Am I a person created in the image of God or am I a product of chance and time? My response to these questions will greatly impact what I allow to happen to myself as well as to others. If God created man in His image, then the commandment "You shall not kill" has meaning; but if man is merely a product of chance and time (as some moderns believe), then killing is an action, like any other action, that must be judged on pragmatic grounds.[9]

The Christian view of human beings is that we are made in the image of God and are to have dominion over the rest of creation (Gen. 1:26). Humans are unique in that we have a self-consciousness and an ability to reason, to create, and to love freely, much like God does. Humans also have the capacity for fellowship with God and with each other. The starting point in relationships, then, is the development of a self-understanding. It is almost impossible to enjoy a meaningful relationship with others or with God when you are not open and honest about yourself. Self-knowledge is not easy. We work at it throughout life. We have developed a variety of different devices for running away from ourselves. John Gardner writes:

> We can keep ourselves so busy, fill our lives with so many diversions, stuff our heads with so much knowledge, involve ourselves with so many people and cover so much ground that we never have time to probe the fearful and wonderful world within. The result is that by middle life most of us are accomplished fugitives from ourselves.[10]

When children are very young and are learning new things, every day, at a phenomenal rate, they are also experiencing great failures. They just keep on trying and never seem to allow these failures to discourage them. By the time they are youth, they have developed an aversion to failure and are less willing to take risks. "By middle age most of us carry in our heads a tremendous catalog of things we have no intention of trying again because we tried them once and failed."[11] One of the immense challenges we face in adult Christian education is to convince our people that they must keep on risking failure if they want to keep learning and growing. This means that leaders of adults must be willing to lead their people through situations where failure is possible. The 21st-century Church will be greatly dependent on daring, risk-taking leaders if the Church is to remain vital and dynamic.

One of the things I am learning as a middle-aged person is the value of solitude. In my moments of solitude I do not try to escape from myself, but I try to be open and better understand who I am. I am discovering that you do not have to withdraw to some remote place like the mountains, forests, lakes, or deserts to find solitude. Solitude does not depend on physical isolation. You can find solitude right in your own house or workplace. You can find solitude in the center of a big city, in the middle of a large crowd, in the context of a very active and busy life, or while riding along the highway in your automobile. Solitude is a matter of the heart. "To live a spiritual life," writes Nouwen, "we must first find the courage to enter into the desert of our loneliness and to change it by gentle and persistent efforts into a garden of solitude."[12] For the past 10 years of my life, I have kept a journal. I can honestly say that this has been one of the richest and most rewarding of any spiritual disciplines I have ever accepted. Those moments of solitude when I can "journal" my inmost feelings and thoughts and prayers are some of my most treasured moments. I do not feel any compulsion to journal every day, and if I miss a day or a week, I do not feel guilty. What I have discovered, however, is that I am often drawn by strong desire to talk to the Lord in that journal. It has proven to be a source of great spiritual blessing. I would highly recommend it as an opportunity for spiritual discipline for the busy people who are moving toward the 21st century.

John Wesley, himself a journaler, reminds us, however, that there is no such thing as a solitary religion. To be truly and fully Christian, we must find ways to move out in relationship to others. The family is one of the crucial groups to whom we are responsible. So much seems to be happening in society to destroy the family. Some are even predicting the dissolution of the family as we know it in the 21st century. Christians are committed to strong families. The family is that balanced environment designed by God to nurture and grow human beings. We must not allow the family to be weakened any more than it already is. "If the family fails, then all the other institutions of society will fail." The future of the nation is not going to be settled by congressmen or ambassadors or presidents but by parents.[13] It is encouraging to see churches beginning to put their money into building "family life centers" to bring the families of their church and community together. A church moving toward the 21st century that does not fund and promote and emphasize family ministry is also moving toward self-destruction.

As critically important as the family is, we must not allow ourselves to become isolated family units. This may be our greatest temptation in the 21st century. The local community of believers meeting together for Bible study and fellowship and worship is the New Testament pattern for us. As Ross Snyder reminds us, "In a most immediate way we hunger for a group of people who believe in one another and in something together, who have symbols and ways of making sense out of life. Whatever we might name it to ourselves, we hunger for the body of Christ."[14] One way to rediscover this hunger for the local church is to be laid up in the hospital or a sickbed at home for weeks with no opportunity to worship with the church family.

The most important of all our relationships is our relationship with God. This relationship involves realizing our own inadequacy and sin and reaching out to God, who can help us. "We need the willingness and courage to reach out far beyond the limitations of our fragile and finite existence toward our loving God in whom all life is anchored."[15] Life needs an anchor; life needs a center. To anchor your life in another human person, in your job, or in yourself is to set yourself up for disappointment and failure. Only the sovereign God of the universe, the Center and Anchor of all reality, is worthy of our complete trust and confidence. He is that broader, deeper, and higher reality on whom we can stake our very lives. The New Age movement is running rampant in our modern world. It urges people to look within to discover God. When you look inward, they claim, lo and behold you discover that *you are God.*

The Bible, however, teaches that God is beyond our human hearts and minds, beyond our thoughts and feelings, beyond our expectations and desires, and beyond all the events and experiences that make up our lives; yet He is the Center of it all. We can receive Him by faith in Jesus Christ as our Lord and Savior. We can commune with Him through prayer. When we reach out to God in prayer, we are pulled away from our own self-preoccupations and are pushed into a new world that cannot be contained within the narrow boundaries of our mind and heart.[16] We are ushered into the wonderful world of relationship with the Heavenly Father.

John Stott is right. "Only a return to the living God who created us, sustains us and can remake us through Christ . . . can enable us, with confidence and without fear, to look forward to the year 2000 A.D."[17]

A Theology of Callings

This is an attempt to answer the question, "What should I

do?" The Shorter Westminster Catechism asks the question like this: "What is the chief end of man?" John Calvin answered the question, "The chief end of man is to glorify God and to enjoy Him forever."[18]

The question of "vocation" or "calling" is one of our most crucial questions. Youth and young adults struggle with it, but it is a recurring question for many at middle age and retirement. So many people are unhappy with what they do. Someone once asked, "Who works harder, the ditch digger or the medical doctor? The answer is, the person who hates his job more."[19] The point is, if you hate what you are doing, it is all hard work.

There are at least two ways to view your vocation: choice or calling. The choice approach simply means that individuals decide or make a choice to do a certain job. It is just a personal decision to go a certain way. The individuals may *not* have the gifts or talents required to do the job effectively. They may not have the training or any experience to do the job. They may even discover that it is not a very enjoyable job, but they try to survive doing it anyway. Maybe a father pushed his son to carry on the business or the family farm when the son could really care less about the job; but out of respect or in response to pressure or under a grossly unrealistic self-appraisal, the son decides to try. These people often work very hard but are also very tired and almost never satisfied with who they are or what they do. "Many of us will never be truly happy or fulfilled," writes Bob Benson, "because we never succeed in becoming ourselves. We never get around to being the particular person or painter we were intended to be. We live our lives painting someone else's picture."[20]

The calling approach involves choice but is more than choice. This approach takes into account who you are—your background, your gifts and talents, your training. The Christian person even goes so far as to ask, "Is this what God wants me to do with my life?" These people work in response to a divine call that they believe and feel God has given them. With a few exceptions, the majority of people who are "called people" work at a task they enjoy, using the gifts and abilities with which God has endowed them, and tend to find much meaning and fulfillment in their vocation. This is *not* to say that they like everything they do or always feel successful. It is to say that they have learned to make peace with the routine. Gordon MacDonald reminds us, "Because most of life is lived in routine, the man or woman who learns to make peace with routine responsibilities and obligations will make the greatest contributions in the long run."[21]

Philip Clarke Brewer's little poem called "Five Loaves and Two Fishes" is a beautiful description of calling:

> God uses
> what you have
> to fill a need which
> you never could have filled.
>
> God uses
> where you are
> to take you where
> you never could have gone.
>
> God uses
> what you can do
> to accomplish what
> you never could have done.
>
> God uses
> who you are
> to let you become who
> you never could have been.[22]

The person whose vocation selection was by the choice approach has a tendency to say, "Look what I have done. I am a self-made person. I did it all myself and in my own way." The person whose vocation selection was by the calling approach has a tendency to say, "Look what God has done through me. He gave me the health and wisdom and strength to accomplish this feat. The credit goes to Him!" This is part of the meaning in Hannah Whitall Smith's excellent statement:

> A religion of bondage always exalts self. It is what I do—my efforts, my wrestlings, my faithfulness. But a religion of liberty leaves self nothing to glory in; it is all Christ, and what He does, and what He is, and how wonderfully He saves.[23]

This is not to say that we should never take any credit and should only view ourselves as poor, worthless worms. It is, rather, to say that our vocation is to give God the glory. How critical it will be for adults in the 21st century to understand the meaning of vocation and calling in a rapidly changing world!

A Theology of Truths

This is an attempt to answer the question, "What is important?" As we move toward the end of the 20th century, we are living in a period of time when nothing appears to be nailed down. Nothing is for sure; everything is up for grabs. The world seems to have turned completely away from the Bible and is running madly in every direction. Self-proclaimed "saviors" are making rules and crowning them with divine status. People do not seem to know what to believe and what *not* to believe.

The time has come for Christian believers to stand up and tell the truth! The world needs to hear that the Bible is the divine Revelation of God to mankind. They need to hear that the Bible is the Word of God, that the Bible is the truth, and that the truth will set you free (John 8:32).

The true Church of the living God, made up of true believers from many different denominations, seems to be surrounded on all four sides by clouds of fuzzy and confusing versions of the truth. (See the chart below.) On one side are the scandal-ridden media churches and televangelists whose desperate clamor for funds, deplorable ethics, and strange theatrics overshadow any gospel truth they might have been able to present. On a second side are the New Agers and the cults with their grains of truth mixed with heresy. These have a low view of Jesus and the Bible. They are so aggressive and so committed, and many are growing so rapidly, that many in the world are convinced they must have the truth. A third side contains the liberal church. They have the traditions and the money and the respectability, but they have left their first love and sound doctrine and are dying at an alarming rate. They could once again be purveyors of the truth, as some of them were, but that is all in the past. On the fourth side is the secular or pagan world. They reject God and the Bible and promote a purely humanistic and materialistic world. There are no absolutes. Reality and truth and values are what you decide they are.

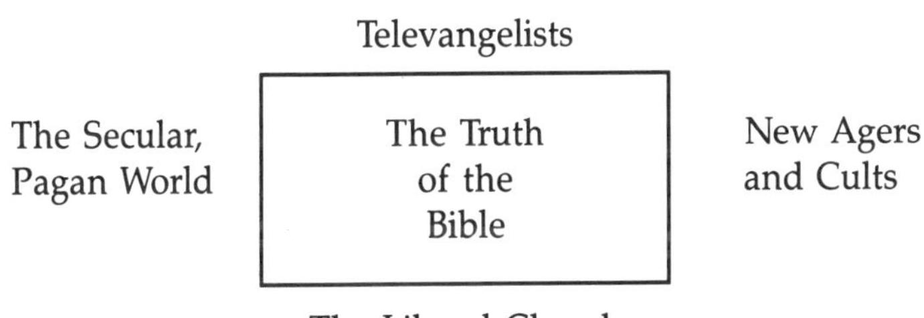

There has never been a revival of religion in the history of the world (to my knowledge) that was not first nurtured in a revival of Bible study. No greater legacy could we leave the adults of the 21st century than that of a renewed love for and greater understanding of the Bible.

A Theology of Directions

This is an attempt to answer the question, "Where am I going?" It is a question regarding the journey of life and its destination.

Abraham answered the call of God to leave the security of his home and move to the insecurity of a new land. The Lord pointed the direction, and Abraham followed. "By faith Abraham, when called to go to a place he would later receive as his inheritance, obeyed and went, even though he did not know where he was going" (Heb. 11:8).

The Bible reminds us that there was a beginning and that there will be a consummation or ending. We are not on an eternal merry-go-round. We are *not* bound to some endless cycle of birth-life-death-reincarnation. History is going somewhere. God is involved in time and space. We are all on a pilgrimage. It is a journey that began in my heart at my house and will end at His house. God has assured His followers that He will be with us always, even, "to the very end of the age " (Matt. 28:20). So our pilgrimage is not a matter of aimless wandering. "We are moving through life, from God, with God, to God, within God's purposes. There is a destination to which we all travel."[24] It is not a journey without its jars, shocks, surprises, sudden turns, and suffering. But it is a good journey with much opportunity for discovery and becoming. Both the journey and the destination are to be treasured. Sometimes, in the providence of God, incredibly great things emerge out of the shocks and hardships of the journey.

The story of Ludwig van Beethoven is such a journey. Beethoven was a promising young piano virtuoso and composer. He discovered, to his great dismay, that he was going deaf. At first he did not want anybody to know, so he tried to conceal his affliction. It became so bad that he eventually gave up playing the piano in public and cut himself off from everybody except his intimate friends. He became so depressed that he cried out in anguish about his unfortunate condition. He had come to a crossroads in his journey and needed *new directions.* Beethoven made a choice. The deafness sent him to composing music with a passion he had not known before. He began to commune with his spirit and sought solace in nature. Now that he was deaf, he could not hear music anymore, so he tried to capture the majestic and turbulent chords that he could hear within himself. In rapid succession, Beethoven composed a series of masterpieces that remain with us today as classics. What happened? Out of his suffering emerged new directions and new energies.[25]

We have good reason to hope and believe that out of the bewilderment and confusion of the contemporary scene will emerge some new directions for the Church of the 21st century.

"We theologize," says Ross Snyder, "because we are driven to do so by the day-to-day struggle to survive."[26] If our program of adult Christian education is to survive into the new millennium, we must theologize. As we struggle to find answers to these critical theological questions, we begin to create our own future. We set in place certain parameters and presuppositions that will become the framework for the future. It is almost as if the future becomes (with God's help) self-fulfilling prophecy.

Toffler believes that three basic requirements are necessary for the civilization of tomorrow: (1) The need for *community,* (2) the need for *structure,* and (3) the need for *meaning.*[27] What institutions are best designed to meet these three needs? The answer is obvious. They are the institutions God created and intended to provide community, structure, and meaning—*the home and the church.* This is the exciting thought! The disturbing thought is that these institutions on which society depends (marriage, home, family, church) seem to be crumbling.

There are no more significant agenda items for our future than the strengthening of these institutions: marriage, home, family, and church.

Harvey Cox is right. "The failure of modern theology is that it continues to supply plausible answers to questions that fewer and fewer people are asking."[28] The success of our adult Christian education programs in the future will greatly depend on how effectively we can deal with these critical questions: From where did I come? Why am I here? Who am I? What should I do? What is important? Where am I going? Our ability to speak to these questions from the Scriptures will be one of the most significant ministries we could provide for adults.

4

A Mandate for Adult Education

Just how necessary is adult education to the future of the local church? We have proceeded to give demographic reasons (chap. 1), cultural reasons (chap. 2), and theological reasons (chap. 3) for doing adult education in the church. These are good and valid arguments, but what does the Word of God have to say about it? Is the Christian education of adults a take-it-or-leave-it matter in Scripture?

In many ways, the Bible is a book for adults. It was written by adults, and for the most part, it was written to the adult. Of course, it is true that even a child or youth can study and understand enough of its incredible truth to be saved; yet to grasp all of its concepts and the full sweep of the message of redemption requires a certain maturity. The writer of Hebrews says, "But solid food is for the mature, who by constant use have trained themselves to distinguish good from evil" (5:14). The goal of the Bible, then, is to help God's people to "grow up . . . and become mature" (Eph. 4:15, 13).

In an attempt to present a mandate for adult education, I want to highlight what appear to me to be "the five critical tasks of the church." The church can choose to do many good, legitimate things, but these are some things it *must* do in order to be an authentic New Testament church. These are the bottom-line, irreducible, lowest-common-denominator tasks. It seems to me that everything a church should do can be incorporated under one of the following tasks. (See the chart below.) Not only do these serve as church tasks, but they also serve as tasks for the adult education program of the church.

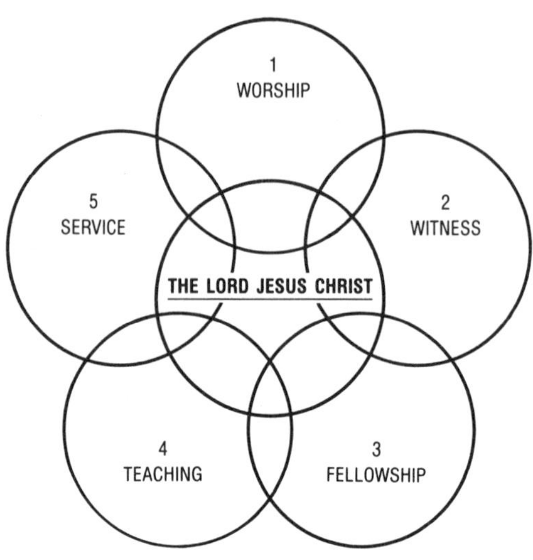

Worship

This is the place to start: learning to "reach up" in worship. Some should learn to lead in worship, but all should be trained to worship. It is difficult to witness effectively, teach, fellowship, or serve until you have first worshiped. A. W. Tozer, a great evangelical preacher, preached a message on worship in which he said: "Worship is the missing jewel of the evangelical church."[1] Many evangelicals agree with Tozer that our worship is a weak area. "We are the strongest in areas of evangelism, teaching, and fellowship," writes Robert Webber of Wheaton

College. "We are improving greatly in the area of servanthood . . . and the ministry of healing . . . But depth in the area of worship is badly lacking."[2]

Worship is both private and public. A person needs to develop personal spiritual disciplines and then encourage their development in others. We should focus on such spiritual disciplines as prayer, devotional reading, meditation, fasting, journaling, and celebration. The power of praise and the inspiration of our great hymnology should be an integral part of our worship training. Charles Wesley's great hymn, "Love Divine, All Loves Excelling" ends with a most memorable definition of worship: "Lost in wonder, love, and praise." That's the essence of all true worship.

One reason there are so many bored, fatigued, unhappy, unfulfilled people in many evangelical churches is that we have forgotten how or never learned how to "reach up" in worship. Many of us simply do not know _how_ to worship.

The Early Church engaged in prayer, fasting, praise, singing, and great celebrations of joy. Here is some evidence of worship in the Book of Acts:

1. They prayed together often (1:14; 2:42-43).
2. They fasted and prayed (13:2-3).
3. They sang and prayed (16:25).
4. They praised God together (2:47).
5. They were greatly joyful (8:8; 13:52; 16:34).

There is little doubt that worship is a part of the biblical mandate for a New Testament church. True worship, however, flies in the face of much that our secular world promotes. Those living in the fast lanes of a pagan society are led to believe that meaning is to be found in busyness, noise, exotic experiences, new tastes and smells, and more and more stuff. Many of us are discovering that the fast-lane approach is not the way to power in the inner spirit. Mother Teresa agrees. She says:

> We need to find God and he cannot be found in noise and restlessness. God is the friend of silence. See how nature—trees, flowers, grass—grow in silence; see the stars, the moon and sun, how they move in silence . . . The more we receive in silent prayer, the more we can give in our active life.[3]

Thomas Kelly encourages the believer to make worship a part of the whole day. "Let inward prayer be your last act before you fall asleep," he writes, "and the first act when you awake."[4]

Worship, then is a critical task of the church and of the adult ministries program.

Witness

Learning to reach out is also crucial, but we must first reach up to God in worship and receive renewal and resourcing from Him. Reaching out is what believers do when they witness. Witnessing means identifying with the Cause, telling the Good News, and leading others to the Lord and to the Church.

Preaching is one of the primary ways this is done. A preacher is one who heralds or proclaims the Word of God. At Pentecost, Peter stood up, "raised his voice," and preached to the crowd. He quoted from the Hebrew Scriptures (Joel 2:28-32; Ps. 16:8-11; 110:1), and then he preached Christ to the people and pleaded with them to be saved. About 3,000 responded to his invitation and were converted that day (Acts 2). R. T. Kendall, a British pastor, recently delivered lectures on preaching at Southwestern Baptist Theological Seminary. He warned preachers against preaching "at" the people. To preach "at" the people is cowardice. To preach "for" the people is performance. To preach "down to" the people is arrogance. To preach "up to" the people is fear. The proper approach is to preach "to" the people, which is transaction between preacher and people. Both are involved.[5]

Revivals are a traditional tool that evangelical churches have used effectively in reaching out to the lost. Personal evangelism has been an effective method ever since Andrew found his brother Simon Peter and told him, "We have found the Messiah" (John 1:41).

Missions is an equally effective tool of witness. Missions means a willingness to give a cup of cold water in Jesus' name. Some give this cup of water in their neighborhood. Others have a mission to the great, sprawling urban and inner-city areas of the world. Still others are involved in "saltwater missions" and invest portions of their lives as witnesses in another culture and other world areas.

One of our most effective outreach tools has fallen by the wayside in recent years. We used to emphasize it, but we have nearly stopped talking about it. I refer to the common Christian ministry of witnessing or sharing your faith. F. F. Bruce claims that the Book of Acts can be summed up in five words: "You will be my witnesses" (1:8).[6] Acts 1:8 forms an outline for the whole Book of Acts:

Chapters 1—7	Witnessing to Jerusalem
Chapters 8:1—11:18	Witnessing to all Samaria and Judea
Chapters 11:19—28:31	Witnessing to the whole world

An eyewitness is a person who was there and has first-hand knowledge of an event. The disciples and women who walked with Jesus all the way to the tomb were eyewitnesses. A true witness is one who tells the truth and lives the truth. A false witness is one who twists the truth or tells or lives a lie. A verbal witness is one who talks with another person about his faith in Christ. There are many people who talk but are not true witnesses, and there are many "witnesses" who do not talk. The silent witness is a person's reliance on behavior and life-style to communicate his faith in Christ.

The Book of Acts gives somes hints on witnessing:
1. Start in your own neighborhood (1:8).
2. Pray for boldness to witness (4:29).
3. Simply relate what you have personally experienced (4:20).
4. Continue to witness (verbally and silently) through life (4:33).
5. Witnessing always means telling "the good news" (11:20).

The key to keeping a church from becoming stagnant, sterile, and self-satisfied is found in reaching out and bearing witness through preaching, evangelism, missions, and simply sharing the faith. Some Christians sing; others teach; a few preach; but *all Christians witness.* It is nonnegotiable. We witness by what we say, what we do, what we don't do, how we react, where we go, where we choose not to go, how we work, how we play, and how we worship. "The church is never powerful unless she can produce her witnesses."[7] There is something about a "cloud of witnesses" that gives us courage to go on (Heb. 12:1).

My pastor told of an old man who was crawling across a frozen lake. Down on his hands and knees, he was timidly reaching out to see if the ice would hold. As he gingerly inched along, he was worrying about getting to the middle of the lake and the ice giving way. Suddenly, as he crept along, he was startled by a loud clanging and saw a farmer driving a big wagon and team of horses out across the frozen lake. Obviously the farmer had been over the lake before and knew it would hold. Embarrassed, the man got up and began to walk. Knowing that someone had gone before and made it gave him courage to walk on. Our witness very often is a source of courage for the spiritually weak, and it can give them courage to walk on.

The Christian adults of the 21st century will doubtless need the special power of the Holy Spirit to enable them to witness with boldness. The time could come when the Supreme Court would not only banish prayer and Bible reading in the schools but also deny Christians the opportunity to witness in the community. Like the Sanhedrin in Acts, they might say, "We gave you strict orders *not* to teach in this name" (5:28, italics added). Hopefully there will be some powerful Christian witnesses somewhere who will demonstrate a courage born of the Spirit and who will say, "We must obey God rather than men!" (5:29), and, "We cannot help speaking about what we have seen and heard" (4:20).

Teach

Learning to teach and training others to teach is another critical New Testament task. You cannot keep the Great Commission without teaching: "Go and make disciples . . . *teaching* them to obey everything I have commanded you. And surely I am with you always, to the very end of the age" (Matt. 28:19-20, italics added).

Paul, in an attempt to assure that the teaching ministry would continue to thrive in the Early Church, exhorted Pastor Timothy: "And the things you have heard me say in the presence of many witnesses entrust to reliable men who will also be qualified to teach others" (2 Tim. 2:2).

The Early Church considered teaching a matter of daily importance. They were devoted to it. Here are some examples from Acts of their teaching commitment:

1. They were devoted to the apostles' teaching (2:42).
2. The apostles were teaching the people (4:2).
3. They taught in the Temple courts (5:21, 25).
4. They never stopped teaching from house to house (5:42).

5. Philip explained the scripture to the Ethiopian (8:35).
6. Barnabas and Saul taught great numbers of people at the church (11:26).
7. Paul taught for a year and a half at Corinth (18:11).
8. Apollos taught at Ephesus (18:25).
9. Paul taught at Rome for two years (28:30-31).

That was the Early Church. What about the ministry of teaching today? Bishop Wilke believes there is a great openness to the message of the Bible today. "I have never seen people so hungry to know and understand the Bible as they are today," he claims. "Across the country, in little towns and in cities, groups are gathered with their Bibles open to read, talk, discuss and pray."[8]

There are at least three activities involved in teaching:

1. *Instruction.* This means transmitting the facts of the faith from generation to generation. It involves understanding what God's Word has to say to me in my life today. Wilke says: "The Bible is our book, and we will carry it into the future with us. We will teach it to our people, and they in turn will teach it to others."[9] A person, in any generation, needs to know a certain amount of Bible facts in order to make a spiritual value judgment. We will not be able to afford biblical illiteracy in the 21st-century Church. It could do us in.

2. *Indoctrination.* This is a bad word in contemporary society. It means to inspire people to adopt Christian values, exhibit Christian attitudes, express Christian emotions, and be loyal to the cause of Christ. I, for one, believe it is high time we stop apologizing for our task of indoctrination and start doing it effectively. Children, youth, and adults all need to be inspired to be Christian in every realm of their living. The adults of the 21st century will desperately need to know Christian doctrine and be able to "give the reason for the hope" that they have (1 Pet. 3:15).

3. *Training.* This involves leading our people to develop skills in worship, reaching, teaching, fellowship, and service. There will always be the need to teach people to pray, praise, study, meditate, memorize, sing, testify, preach, teach, lead, encourage, give, and embody the faith. A "state of the art training program" would be one of the most thoughtful and helpful investments we could make in the future.

I am intrigued by Bishop Wilke's conclusions for his own Methodist church. He discusses in his very honest book *And Are We Yet Alive?* the reasons he believes his church is suffering such damaging losses. Then he looks to the future and becomes prophetic:

> The twenty-first century belongs to lay Christians and to preachers who know how to teach them. In the decades ahead, the minister's task will be critical, not because ministers must run faster and do more, but because they will be called upon to inspire, to convert, to train and to build the community as never before.[10]

Teaching is a matter of "reaching down," reaching down below the surface to understand God's truth. It also means coming down off any pedestal one is on and accepting the vulnerable role of teacher.

Fellowship

This is the "reach inward" to put your arms around others and help them to grow and mature. Fellowship is not something we do or don't do. It is not a thing or a life-style. It is much more than getting together. Just getting together will not magically create fellowship. We call it fellowship because of the One whom we share in common. It is the fact that we are "in Christ" that we can have fellowship.

The Early Church is our model of fellowship. It is true that togetherness encourages or makes it convenient for fellowship to occur. The disciples in Acts were:

1. together in prayer (1:14)
2. together in one place (2:1)
3. together with other believers (2:44)
4. together in the Temple (2:46)
5. together for meals in their houses (2:46)
6. together in heart and mind (4:32)

They seemed to just get together and enjoy the presence of the Lord. One common thread in all the examples listed above is "commonness"—commonly shared realities. What or whom they shared together was more important than mere physical or geographical togetherness. Common faith in Christ, common loyalties, common purposes, a common code of conduct—this is what draws us together. Not who we are nor what we do, but whom we share and what we share in common—this is fellowship. It is this from which we draw healing, strength, encouragement, and release. It is this that impresses the world. This is why true Christian believers—Baptist, Methodist, Presbyterian, Nazarene, Assembly of God, or whatever—can actually have a wonderful fellowship, simply because they have a common participation in Christ. One reason why fellowship is so helpful to us might be illustrated by this saying from the works of John of the Cross: "The virtuous soul that is alone and without a master, is like a lone burning coal: it will grow colder rather than hotter . . . consider how much more can be accomplished by two together than by one alone."[11]

This beautiful prayer for fellowship could be our prayer for each other as well as for the Church of the 21st century:

> O God, you have made us for fellowship, and have given us the power both to help and harm our fellows. Grant us the wisdom to know what is their good, and the ready will to help them to attain it. Heal those we have wounded, strengthen those whom we have failed, grant us all your healing grace, and make our fellowship to be your family, through Jesus Christ our Lord. Amen.[12]

Serve

The final critical task of the Church is the "reach around." This involves all the social ministries, the healing ministries, and the stewardship ministries. It is at this very point that the Christian faith really begins to make sense for most people. It begins to fit together as we are able to embody it and live it out in our lives.

We become instruments of healing and deliverance as we give of our time, talents, and money to others. We become stewards of our bodies, marriages, families, and resources. We give of ourselves without resentment. Touching human hurt with no eye to who gets the credit is our motivation. We can literally reach around the needs of others (especially the hurting, and you need not look far because most people are hurting) and become healing to them.

A few years ago I invited a young widow named Cheryl to my college Christian education of adults class. The class was questioning her about how she and her three young children had coped since her husband had been suddenly killed in a farming accident. Her answers were not what they expected. One aspiring young pastor said, "Cheryl, I guess the Bible really meant a lot to you when you found out about your husband's death, didn't it?" She replied, "No, I was so hurt I could not read it!" Another said, "Surely you were able to find comfort in prayer?" Again with all honesty, she replied, "No, not at all! I couldn't pray because I was so shocked and so numb!" The class sat in stunned silence for a while. She then told us what many of the church people had (in all good conscience) said to her: "Cheryl, you just call me if there is anything I can do for you." "But," Cheryl said, "I never did!" Her message to that class was this: When you are really devastated by grief, your greatest need is simply to have someone to BE THERE! (I call it "the ministry of being there.")

This is what it means to give yourself to the ministry of reaching around another. Many moderns salve their guilty consciences by offering money to the hurting. "Money is a cheap substitute for human caring," says Colson. "Being there is what matters."[13]

The Book of Acts gives indisputable evidence to support the critical task of giving. The pattern of giving in Acts included the following:

1. They were inclusive in their giving (2:45).
2. They gave the healing power of Jesus (3:6).
3. They gave stuff (4:32).
4. They gave spiritual witness (4:33).
5. They gave generously (10:2).
6. They gave proportionately (11:29-30).

Thomas Aquinas once called upon Pope Innocent III when the pope was counting a large sum of money. "You see, Thomas," said the pope, "the church can no longer say, 'Silver and gold have I none.'" "True, Holy Father," said Aquinas, "and neither can she now say, 'Rise up and walk!'"[14] Something to think about!

The evidences of healing in Acts are throughout. Chapter 3:6-10 tells the story of Peter being the instrument of healing for the crippled beggar at Gate Beautiful. Chapter 5:12-16 describes crowds of people bringing their sick and ends with the triumphant note that "all of them were healed." Chapter 8:7-8 tells of the exorcisms in Samaria of many evil spirits and of the healings of many paralytics and cripples. Because of this ministry of healing "there was great joy in that city" (v. 8).

The evidences of "ministries of encouragement" are everywhere in Acts:

1. It is a personal gift or trait (4:36).
2. The Holy Spirit is an encourager (9:31).
3. A group is encouraged (11:23).

4. Even unbelievers want encouragement (13:15).
5. New Christians need encouragement (14:22).
6. Some letters and speeches encourage (15:31-32).
7. Encourage another after you experience victory (16:40).
8. Encourage individual persons in private (18:27).
9. Speak words of encouragement (20:1-2).
10. Encourage when the storm is raging (27:22, 25).
11. Learn to receive encouragement (28:15).

This ministry of serving (giving, healing, encouraging) is summed up in a beautiful statement attributed to the Quaker, William Penn: "I expect to pass through life but once. If, therefore, there be any kindness I can show, or any good thing I can do to any fellow-being, let me *do it now,* and not defer or neglect it, as I shall not pass this way again."[15]

It seems to me that the Bible is clear regarding the *vital necessity* of a Christian education program for adults. It is *not* a take-it-or-leave-it matter. It is critical! The Word of God mandates that we teach, or we cannot call ourselves a New Testament church—whether we live in the 1st century or the 21st century.

5

The Shape of Adult Sunday School

In light of the demographics (chap. 1), culture (chap. 2), theology (chap. 3), and biblical tasks (chap. 4), what can we do to shape a viable program of 21st-century adult Christian education? Some pessimists would say, "Junk the Sunday School! Get rid of adult classes." Those churches who have tried that have been unable to find a replacement. As a result, they have suffered great losses and are caught in a whirlpool of indecision as the new century approaches.

The truth of the matter is that Sunday School, with all its problems, is still a powerful religious movement. It began at the hands and in the hearts of laypersons (men and women). It has been kept alive by laypersons. Its future rests (to a great extent) with laypersons. It really is an authentic lay movement. Unless something unforeseen occurs, the Sunday School will make the transition into the 21st century. We will find it there in some shape. But this will depend considerably on what we (especially laypersons) decide that its shape should be.

Chapters 5 and 6 will reflect a number of my own experiences and perceptions as a teacher and worker with teachers.

Adult Sunday School classes come in a variety of "colors"—like the colors of the rainbow. Some are bright and cheery like the warmer colors; others are dark and cold like the colder colors. Some are attractive and appealing; others are depressing and foreboding.

And adult classes come in various "shapes." Some are boxed in, self-contained, and narrow like a square or rectangle. They may have been together for several years and have become exclusive. It's almost impossible to break through into their shrinking little fellowship circle. You must serve a probationary period and prove yourself worthy of their fellowship before they will let you in. They may still enjoy good fellowship and high-quality Bible study, but these classes tend to become stagnant and stop growing. What they do is to maintain their group, and that is not unimportant.

Other classes are shaped like a circle. They are open and inviting and receptive to new people. Often these are the newer and less-established classes. They are much more inclusive and willing to assimilate new people into their ranks. Their fellowship circle is large and growing. To remain open and inclusive, a class must consciously determine that they will not allow themselves to become narrow. Although the natural evolution of classes is to plateau and become stagnant, this condition can be held off for years, but it requires a concerted effort by the class as a whole.

Groups

What kinds of people choose to attend adult Sunday School classes? Are there distinguishable groups who come? The following is a discussion of four groups that consitute most adult classes.

1. *Those seeking answers.* Believe it or not, some come to Sunday School in quest of answers to the ultimate questions of their lives. They really want to know what the Bible has to say about life and living and life hereafter. They are also prime

candidates for practical answers for becoming better mates, better parents, better persons, better neighbors, better churchmen, and better workers. In many cases, these persons are the most mature persons in the church. They attend Sunday School regularly and predictably. They come, whether the regular teacher is there or not. They attend worship even when the pastor is on vacation. It's not the teacher or the pastor who motivate them to participate in Bible study; rather, it is a deep yearning to know more of God's truth. They continue to come not just because they are being fed, but because they are feeding themselves on the Word of God and on the fellowship of the group.

Sometimes it is infant or baby Christians who complain about not being fed. Mature adult Christians have learned how to feed themselves.

2. *Those seeking affirmation.* These people come to Sunday School class with a totally different motivation—to receive strokes, to be affirmed, to visit, talk, shake hands, hug, laugh, and fellowship. They have an almost overwhelming need to be "noticed and nurtured." These are the ones who are easily offended if someone does not sit with them and they are forced to sit alone in the class. The very reason they came was to sit by somebody who would pay attention to them. These are the ones who may not return next Sunday if they feel no one speaks to them. They desperately need a personal touch. More than knowledge or answers to questions, they need friendship and fellowship. They crave warmth, acceptance, kindness, a smile, a handshake, or a hug. They are so caught up in the basic need for affirmation that they cannot even begin to seriously consider the ultimate questions of life.

I recently received a letter from a man who had been a member of the Sunday School class I was teaching. He and his wife had been members for a year or more. The tone of his letter was one of hurt. "My wife and I have decided to attend another class," he began. "It is nothing personal against you as the teacher, but we feel like nobody notices whether we are present or not. Few people speak to us. Nobody has ever invited us over for coffee or for dinner." They left.

Many times these persons have been hurt or wounded and are bleeding emotionally. They need the healing benefits of a warm and accepting group. They really need a class. A healthy class should provide for both the truth seeker and the affirmation seeker. Unless the class is too large and unmanageable, I see no reason why we cannot provide for both. It is the pull of personal warmth and affection that gets these people to class.

3. *Those seeking affiliation.* The question this group is asking is, "Who is in the class?" or "Who is the teacher?" They are looking for a group; they are looking for identity. It must be a group with interests and ambitions similar to theirs. Certain individuals may be in the group whom they would like to get to know better. Some even search for the groups they would like to be seen with or identify with. There may be two drawing cards for these people. The teacher may be someone they admire and respect and with whom they want to study. "Many people 'join a minister' rather than join a church. The same is true in many Sunday School classes," writes Dick Murray. "The longer I live, the more certain I am that I want to go where I am confident the leader has something to give me—if I have a choice."[1] The constituency of the group may also suit them. The lure of the teacher or the lure of the group or both are why they come. People drawn in this way have a deep need to identify with a group or a cause.

4. *Those seeking to do their duty.* It's not really the pull of truth or of affirmation or of the group that motivates these people to attend. It is not necessarily a love for Sunday School either. Why do they come? Although they may not be able to

verbalize why or be willing to admit it, the true reason they attend is duty. In their more sober moments, they would say, "Every Christian *should* go. This is what I *ought* to do. I *must* do this, or the pastor and God will not be pleased with me!" For many who come with this motivation, Sunday School (at its best) is a bore, a drag, and a colossal waste of time. They are often critical of the teacher, the class members, the classroom arrangement, and the curriculum. They come out of habit to "do my duty," but not with a sense of freedom or joy. Their motivation is not to be able to fellowship with a group of people nor to apply God's Word to their lives. Under awful bondage they come to keep from suffering the torture of guilt for failing to do what "I should/ought/must." It is the pull of duty and guilt that gets these people to come.

Purpose

The reasons for having adult Sunday School has been debated for years. The three most common reasons given are (1) outreach, (2) fellowship, and (3) Bible study. I have discussed these for years in my classes, and I usually conclude by revealing my prejudice that Bible study is the best reason; however, having taught an adult class for the last seven years (a class consisting primarily of middle adults) and contemplating the challenges of the 21st century, I am beginning to believe that adult Sunday School needs a fourth element in its statement of purpose—"counsel." I want to address each of these four.

1. *Outreach.* From its beginning, Sunday School has been involved in reaching out and enlisting persons for Bible study. Growing churches still do this. The Sunday School has also been unique as a school because it has sought to lead persons to a personal experience with Jesus Christ, thus incorporating evangelism into Christian education. Many have been con-

verted in or as a result of being in Sunday School. The spiritual dynamic remains a vital part of a healthy class. Unless we continue in some way to reach new people, our Sunday Schools will turn into maintenance meetings, and the Sunday Schools will begin to deteriorate and eventually die. This is already happening in some places. One of the current challenges is reaching persons who already attend worship service, and enlisting them for Bible study (we might call this "inreach").

2. *Fellowship.* Fellowship is especially critical for some and important for everybody. The One we share in common draws us together around the Word of God. "For most people, the fortitude for life does not come from ideas, in and of themselves, but comes instead from people. When God wanted to give us a gift that would give us life, He gave us a life, a person—His Son."[2]

The Sunday School organization is the logical system for organizing for fellowship. Some churches organize "fellowship circles" within the Sunday School classes and find that they usually function best this way. This should be true because most people attend a Sunday School class where they feel most comfortable and with the people with whom they most want to be. Some argue that fellowship is *the only reason* for adult Sunday School.

3. *Bible study.* The strongest single argument for having adult Sunday School is Bible study. Although it is not the only reason, it is (in my humble opinion) *the best reason.* If you do the other two (outreach and fellowship) and never study the Word, you have not had Sunday School. I believe Lyle Schaller is right when he writes, "When the original purpose of the group is redefined to place most or all of the emphasis on 'fellowship,' interest declines. When new members are sought only in the interest of perpetuating the organization, few knock at the door for admission."[3] Bible study must happen. In

some form and at some time, the people must encounter the Bible. This is the primary role and purpose for the ministry of Christian education—to know the truth and be set free (John 8:32)! To study the Bible is really the best reason for expecting adults to come and commit an hour of their valuable time on Sunday mornings.

(4.) *Counsel.* For the first time ever, I am including counsel as a part of the purpose of adult Sunday School. This is because of (what seem to me to be) an almost·overwhelming number of hurts and needs the contemporary adult brings to class. Adults have always carried hurts and had needs, but these seem to be intensifying with the breakdown of the family and Christian values. Personal crises, marriage problems, family stress, parenting pressures, economic difficulties, and spiritual struggles are a part of the baggage the contemporary person carries with him to Sunday School. "Adults come to church with their thoughts clouded by the dark suspicion that their teenagers are on drugs, or that last week's biopsy will reveal malignant tissue," writes Stubblefield, "and the teacher describes the relationship between the Babylonian Ziggurats and the tower of Babel."[4] I have come to the point in my own teaching ministry where I strongly feel that these basic human hurts and needs *must* be addressed. They could very well serve as a guideline for curriculum writers to address; but I am convinced they must serve as the point of departure for teachers of adults. We no longer have the luxury of chasing the children of Israel from Egypt to Canaan for 13 weeks unless we can, in the process, bring the scripture to bear on real human needs. The most successful pastors I know preach to human needs. The most effective teachers of adults I know teach to the needs of their class members. I am not promoting pragmatism, but I am promoting an intensified effort to bring the Bible to bear on common human needs each Sunday. Unless we do, I question whether we have any right to ask adults to come and commit an hour.

I can attest to the fact that on those Sundays when I am enabled by the Holy Spirit to speak to somebody's hurt or need, it is *fun to teach*. When I fail to touch where they are, it is a struggle.

I believe the adult classes of the 21st century will need to be therapeutical and cathartic. We will need to work together to help each other understand and cope with life. What an exciting opportunity this affords us!

The overarching goal of Sunday School, however, is to lead people to begin to embody and live out their faith until they become mature (Eph. 4:13).

Leadership

This 21st century will no doubt bring with it a lot of technological innovations and breakthroughs. These technological advances almost always impact society's institutions. For example, all the elementary schools in our hometown have Apple computers available in the classrooms for teacher and student use. Who knows what future technology will provide for education to use? Who knows how drastically our culture and the world will change? There are, however, those basic needs of adults that persist whatever the age. It is around these needs that the leadership of the adult Sunday School class is organized. The following are 10 key functions that are important to a healthy adult class. In larger classes, a separate person may be available for each function. In smaller classes, one person will need to assume several.

1. *Class leader.* Sometimes called "class president," the class leader gives overall direction to the activities of the class. This can be done by an individual or by a couple (husband and wife may work together to give overall leadership). This person

is the director and coordinator of all class activities and gives direction to planning and evaluating the work of the class.

Another important aspect of this function is the up-front leadership in the actual class session. This individual is the face and personality with whom the class as a whole first identifies when they come into the classroom. The attitude and demeanor of this person is critical to the warmth and acceptance in the class. He can either make or break the feeling of openness to the Bible study leader (teacher) during the teaching period. A clumsy or embarrassing class leader can make it terribly difficult for the teacher to get attention or make teaching-learning happen. A class leader whom the class respects and enjoys will make it easy for the teacher to make the class happen. This is probably the most critical class leadership function aside from the actual teacher. Rather than electing a new one each year, there is a trend to handpick good class leaders and then *reappoint* them from year to year (as we do the teacher).

2. *Bible study leader.* This refers to the teacher. This is, without question, the most critical position of leadership. Very often these are busy people. Too often they are overextended. Increasingly they are experiencing burnout.

This ministry should be performed by one who has proven maturity and who has given some years to studying the Word. It helps if this person is respected by the members of the class and is someone they admire. One does not have to have a degree in Bible or theology to be an effective Bible study teacher. One *does* need to have developed a personal love for a study of and communication of the Word of God.

One could create an almost endless list of qualities for a good teacher of adults. I have chosen to briefly highlight (what seem to me to be) *the five most needful* qualities.

a. *Maturing believer.* The teacher should be not only a Christian but also a maturing Christian. This means that his life is already giving evidence of spiritual sensitiveness and the spiritual disciplines (prayer, Bible study, witness, etc.). This person should be enough of a proven Christian model that new Christians or older Christians would not be led astray if they imitated the way he lives. Proven spiritual sensitivity is most important. A maturing believer can help the class learn to reach up and touch God in personal worship.

(b) *Enthused student.* No teacher with adults should pose as some authority who knows all the answers. Adults know that nobody has all the answers. Instead, the teacher with adults should be an enthusiastic student of the Bible alongside those he teaches—a continuing student in quest, in process of life-long learning. A love for the Word of God, the discipline to study and prepare, and the ability to see how the Bible applies to human lives are valuable qualities for a teacher to possess. A teacher who is an enthused student can help his class members reach down below the surface of the Word of God and of life and learn to eat "solid food" (Heb. 5:14). Teachers of adults need to know that their students have very strong "bunk detectors." They have a highly developed ability to turn their attention on and off and pick and choose. An enthused student of the Word will never resort to "bunk."[5]

(c) *Respected person.* The teacher of adults needs to be a person esteemed, admired, and trusted by the group. Why expect people to support a class taught by someone they distrust or suspect? A proven person of respect is a person who can speak with authority. He is also a person with whom others enjoy fellowshipping. Hopefully, this person of respect likes people and is already a warm and caring person. Usually, such a person of respect is secure enough to be approachable and allow for a creating and releasing class session. A respected person should be able to lead the class to reach inward and experience what it means to have a "healing fellowship."

(d.) *Dedicated storyteller.* A teacher with adults needs to be a proven speaker and communicator. The ability to open windows of light through the telling of great stories is a wonderful and welcome quality to the ears of most adults. There is such "communication dynamic" wrapped up in stories. If you don't believe it, notice what happens to you next Sunday when the pastor gets to his "story." We all tune in! Teachers, like preachers, need to be committed to telling *the* story—the Good News. Whether in class or outside the classroom, the teacher should lead the way in reaching out in witness of what Christ can do for the human heart and life. Adults need someone to talk to them about identity, meaning, marriage, parenting, and vocation. The truth is that we are all participating in writing a story with our lives. We are all a part of the witness.

(e.) *Experienced encourager.* A teacher of adults should already have a track record as a servant and a healer. That is to say, a person who likes people and knows how to minister to and serve others. This person can then lead the class to "reach their arms around" those in the class and community who need their ministry. A "serving teacher" will be an outward-looking, giving encourager of people. He will model the role of moving alongside the needy and ministering to them. This kind of leadership helps to keep the class from becoming selfish and ingrown. "The family of God," writes Swindoll, "is not a place for verbal put-downs, sarcastic jabs, critical comments and harsh judgments."[6] We get enough of this from the world. We need to come together and be encouraged. We all regularly need a breath of fresh air.

A person with these qualities will, while teaching, lead the class toward the fulfillment of the five tasks of the New Testament Church: worship, witness, teach, fellowship, and serve. How important is the teacher? "In the teaching/learning equation," according to Murray, "the teacher is 90%."[7]

3. *Jotters.* A third leadership function that has proven to pay dividends in Sunday School is the ministry of letter writing or note writing. It is very biblical. The apostle Paul popularized it in New Testament times when he wrote notes of encouragement and affirmation to various people and churches.

Contacting visitors, prospects, and absentees is still a critical function in the modern adult class. To receive a personal note or letter is an affirming and motivating experience. It is a way for the class to say, "We care!" or "I care!" This is especially true in a day of so much "junk" mail and "to the occupant or resident" mail. Some people are gifted writers. Try to recruit some of them for this critical ministry.

4. *Phoners.* A more modern means of keeping touch with the people of the adult class is the telephone. We even have the possibility of cellular phones in our automobiles. A phone call is more personal than a card or letter, and it allows opportunity for the recipient to respond. A well-organized cadre of phoners in an adult class can perform quite a significant ministry of caring and keeping touch. A personal call is even more important in the impersonal world of those dreaded (even hated) computer telephone calls.

5. *Callers.* Those who knock on doors and make personal, face-to-face house calls are still important. I know that it is not as easy to catch people at home today. I am also aware that many do not want to be bothered. But there are times when we really need to "be there," on their turf, caring for them. This is *the most personal* of all the caring ministries. Jesus made it a part of His life.

There is a sacrifice of time, but there are also many open doors of opportunity for ministry and for personal evangelism. The results of these calls need to be channeled back to the appropriate person (usually the class leader or his associate) who will keep the group aware of what is going on in the life of the class. The callers are the evangelists of the class who encourage the flow of new blood and new life into the group.

(6) _Spotters._ This refers to a person or persons who are designated to be on the lookout for new people, visitors, or guests and make sure someone greets them and sits with them during class. A visitor should *never* be left to sit alone in your class! It should be someone's responsibility to spot this new person and see that they are properly cared for.

It is quite easy for any social group, such as an adult Sunday School class, to become preoccupied with itself. Class members are often not aware of it, and most would deny it, but they so enjoy being together that they are blinded to walls they have built. Some class members want to be left alone. It takes conscious effort to keep the door really open so that the outsider has a real chance to become an insider.[8]

Too many classes leave this function to chance, to the teacher, or to someone else. This function is too important to be left to chance.

7. _Prayers._ Prayer is just as important to the work of the adult Sunday School class as it is to any other function of the local church—maybe more.

A person could be selected to coordinate a prayer ministry for the needs of the class members. A prayer line or prayer partners could be formed in the class to pray for special needs. Rather than leaving it to chance, a class could organize and make sure that prayer is occurring on a regular basis on behalf of the needs of its members.

(8) _Social conveners._ Adults have social needs, but they vary greatly according to age and social status. I have found, during the last seven years of teaching an adult class, that it is increasingly difficult to mobilize the whole class membership for a social event. Nevertheless, we must try. God created us to be social beings. We need to be together informally, as well as in class.

Select one or more of the most creative, outgoing, and organized persons in the class to give leadership to a class social calendar for a year. I think it is best done a year in advance. Put it on the church calendar. Some try one social event per month. There is a trend, in some locales, to have one big social event per quarter. No healthy adult class can afford to avoid this critical ministry to its members.

9. *Recorders.* The class record or class rolls are an instant portrait of the class. By looking at class records, you can learn a lot about the life or lack of life in a class.

The ministry of record keeping is crucial because there is no good way to keep in touch without some kind of record-keeping procedure. The class records remind us to call, to write, to pray for, to care for, and to reach out to our most valuable resource—those people for whom Christ died! This is not a ministry to be taken lightly.

10. *Compassionate ministries.* These are occasions when special and actual needs will arise in the membership or friendship of the class. Maybe someone will have a crisis or tragedy and will have special need for resources the class as a whole could provide.

To select some caring person from the class to assume responsibility for actual need-meeting ministries can be a real opportunity for service through the class. Such things as taking groceries, providing clothing, and extending emergency child care are common examples of compassionate ministries.

Jesus suggested that doing for others is the same thing as doing for Him (cf. Matt. 25:40). The 21st-century "return home" may mean that the Church will be able to expand some of its teaching ministry back into the home where it all began. Whether we live in the 20th century or the 21st, people will still be in need of the kinds of caring ministries an adult Sunday School class is best equipped to provide. We must be careful, however, not to mistake motion for action (Hemingway). Too many "churches are beehives of random motion, but not of action that will achieve something."[9] The 21st century will likely demand that our action be action that matters and will make a forever difference.

6

A Breath of Fresh Air

My pastor made a classic statement. He wasn't planning to make one; classic statements are seldom planned. It just happened. And I have never forgotten it, although it was spoken over 20 years ago. We were discussing the Sunday School. I asked him, "Just what do you think should happen in a Sunday School class?" His response was, "I think the Sunday School hour should be a breath of fresh air for all those who make an effort to come."

"A breath of fresh air"! I cannot think of any better way to describe what I feel needs to happen in the adult Sunday School class than that—"a breath of fresh air."

What are we talking about when we say, "A breath of fresh air"? Surely this is more than oxygen and hydrogen and nitrogen. Indeed it is! We are really referring to a touch from God, a glimpse into eternity, and a refreshing encounter with the winds of the Holy Spirit.

The First Breath

The first mention of "breath" in the Bible is the breath of God. Gen. 2:7 says, "The Lord God formed the man from the dust of the ground and breathed into his nostrils the breath of life, and the man became a living being." There is something very special about the breath of God. The body of man derived its origin from the dust of the ground, but the soul was breathed from God himself. "Breath" is God's gift to human-kind. God undoubtedly thought man was special because He breathed into man's nostrils and made man a living being. He never did this for an animal. Man became what the Hebrew calls in Gen. 2:7 a *nephesh chayyah* (a living soul or living be-ing). It is *not* as if a "soul" is deposited in man's body. "Man must not be thought of as having a soul; he *is* a soul."[1] One of the really special and distinctive things about man is that he is "God-breathed." This breath of God is more than respiration. It is also life and spirit and inspiration.

The Sustaining Breath

Not only is mankind God-breathed, but we are also sup-ported and sustained by the power of God. His life-giving breath continues to infill and flow into our lives like a breath of fresh air.

The ancient patriarch Job describes the sustaining breath of God like this: "In his hand is the life of every creature and the breath of all mankind" (Job 12:10). Job was keenly aware of the sovereignty of God. He believed the Lord was in control of the universe. On another occasion Job exclaimed, "The Lord gave and the Lord has taken away; may the name of the Lord be praised" (1:21).

The breath of God was the first breath to give us life and to create within us that spiritual capacity to recognize and re-spond to God. There is a human tendency, however, to get busy and grow away from God and get out of breath. More and more we begin to rely on ourselves and our own strength and wisdom. We begin to collect and surround ourselves with toys and stuff. In spite of all our trappings of affluence, we are a culture of self-absorbed, worried, hollow people. Gasping for "a breath of fresh air," we hit bottom before we are forced to look up to the Author of life and breath. An anonymous poet describes our situation in vivid words:

> *One by one He took them from me,*
> *All the things I valued most,*
> *Until I was empty-handed,*
> *Every glittering toy was lost.*
>
> *And I walked earth's highway grieving*
> *In my rags and poverty,*
> *Till I heard His voice inviting,*
> *"Lift your empty hands to Me."*
>
> *So I turned my hands toward heaven,*
> *And He filled them with a store*
> *Of His own transcendent riches,*
> *Till they could contain no more.*
>
> *Then at last I comprehended,*
> *With my stupored mind and dull,*
> *That God could not pour His riches*
> *Into hands already full.*

Periodically we need a few moments of renewal, a new touch, a breath of fresh air. What we are really saying is, "I need God to breathe on me again."

The Life-giving Breath

"The Spirit of God has made me," said Elihu, "the breath of the Almighty gives me life" (Job 33:4). God breathed His life into each of us in a very intimate way. Any vitality, energy, or inner dynamic we possess is a result of His life-giving breath. Ezekiel illustrates this life-giving power in his vision of dry bones. He envisioned the restoration of Israel to the Promised

Land and a rekindling of life within their discouraged hearts. In his vision the Lord said, "I will put breath in you, and you will come to life. Then you will know that I am the Lord" (Ezek. 37:6). The dead, dry, lifeless bones began to rattle and come together; but there was no breath in them, so the Lord said, "'"Come from the four winds, O breath, and breathe into these slain, that they may live."' So . . . breath entered them; they came to life and stood up on their feet—a vast army" (Ezek. 37:9-10).

Many churches and adult classes are dead, dry, and lifeless like these dry bones. No evidence of joy, no celebration, no song. "The pressures of life squeeze out our song," says Swindoll.[2] We live under such excruciating pressure that we cannot muster enough breath or energy to sing our own song. So somebody else is singing our song today. Get in the car, and you will hear it on the radio. Go into the home, the office, the grocery store, the restaurant, the airplane, and the elevator, and you will hear somebody singing your song. You can hardly talk on the telephone without someone saying, "Please hold." While you are holding, guess what? Right! They are singing your song! We need to get our breath back so that we can start singing again. There is nothing we need more than to feel again the life-giving breath of God.

The Last Breath

When a person dies, more than his breathing stops. The person himself dies; life stops. The spirit will live on. The influence or impact of the life may linger, but the life and breath cease. The Psalmist credits the Lord with the giving and taking of breath when he says, "When you take away their breath, they die and return to the dust" (Ps. 104:29).

Made for Two Worlds

The incredible thing about the human being is that he is

made for two worlds. Unlike the other animals, we are created to live and function in two different worlds. To live effectively in the natural world around us, we need to be able to breathe and eat and drink and rest and be safe from harm. To live in "the other world" (the spiritual world) also requires times of rest and nourishment and security as well as periodic breaths of fresh air from the Lord. If we allow ourselves to be cut off from the breath of God, we will wither like fruit on a severed vine.

An animal is made for one world. That animal better make the best of every day because this life is it! There is no more! The human person, however, walks along the dusty roads of earth as a resident of two worlds. Food and water and exercise renew the physical body but are insufficient to renew the spiritual nature of man. The apostle Paul encourages us when he writes, "Though outwardly we are wasting away, yet inwardly we are being renewed day by day" (2 Cor. 4:16).

This earnest human longing for renewal and a breath of fresh air is reflected in the words of a great old hymn of the Church:

> *Breathe on me, Breath of God;*
> *Fill me with life anew,*
> *That I may love what Thou dost love,*
> *And do what Thou wouldst do.*
>
> *Breathe on me, Breath of God,*
> *Until my heart is pure,*
> *Until with Thee I will one will,*
> *To do and to endure.*
>
> *Breathe on me, Breath of God,*
> *Till I am wholly Thine,*
> *Until this earthly part of me*
> *Glows with Thy fire divine.*

> *Breathe on me, Breath of God;*
> *So shall I never die,*
> *But live with Thee the perfect life*
> *Of Thine eternity.*

—EDWIN HATCH

This hymn is a clear recognition of how desperately dependent we really are on the sovereign God of the universe. He is our Life-Giver and our Breath-Maker. The very least we can do is remember to give credit where credit is due. Johann Sebastian Bach understood this. On almost all of his manuscripts, he penned two sets of initials. At the beginning of the piece, he wrote the letters "JJ," and he wrote "SDG" at the end. "JJ" stood for *Jesu juvet* ("Jesus, help me!"). "SDG" meant *Soli deo gloria* ("To God alone be the glory!"). Not a bad idea for us. Begin each day with a "JJ" ("Jesus, help me!") and conclude the day with a "SDG" ("To God alone be the glory!").[3]

A Breathless Society

Look at them as they come to Sunday School and worship. Numbed by living in the fast lane. Bleary-eyed from the blast and bombardment of many hours of television gazing. Depressed by the financial crunch. Hurt by other people. Torn by pressure on the job, turmoil in the home, stress in the marriage, or problems with children. Most everything they have read in the newspapers, heard on the radio, or seen on television has been discouraging. Here they come, trying to look like everything is OK; but just below the surface of their lives is a seething caldron of pressures and stresses almost too heavy to bear. Wounded and bleeding, many of them stumble into Sunday School and church on Sunday mornings. They are tired and almost out of breath. Can you think of anything they need more than a breath of fresh air? A word of hope? A ray of

94

light? A brief glimpse into eternity? A few moments to inhale the cool, clear, mountainlike air of the Word of God? A chance to feel the gentle, springlike rain of the Holy Spirit?

A Breathless Church

The tragedy is that too many churches have coasted along in the latter years of the 20th century. They have become so entangled with culture and caught up in being respectable that their fires are burning dangerously low, and some have already gone out. It brings to mind what happened to the early hunters on safari in Africa. They would build their fires high at night in order to keep the animals in the bush. In the early hours of the morning, the fires would burn low. All around them they could see the approaching outlined shapes of animals and a ring of encircling eyes in the darkness. When the fire was high, they would stay far off; but when the fire was low, the animals approached again.

"As we have witnessed the erosion and breakdown of the Christian culture in the West," writes Os Guinness, "so we have seen the vacuum filled by an upsurge of ideas that would have been unthinkable when the fires of the Christian culture were high."[4] Look around you, and you will see "a ring of encircling eyes" moving in to fill the vacuum left by a once-dynamic Church. These are the eyes of the cults, the occult, the New Age movement, and the atheistic secularists.

Not only have the fires of revival and renewal flickered and gone out, but many churches are fountains gone dry. "Rather than being springs of life-giving energy that cause people to grow and to delight in God's way, they become sources of stress."[5]

Bishop Wilke believes his church became selfish and turned inward. "Our energies and resources are expended internally," he writes. "The machinery of the church receives unbelievable attention; we scurry about oiling the wheels of the organizational structure . . . our structure has become an end in itself."[6]

Is it possible that the adult Sunday School class could again become a receptacle for springs of living water to refresh its people (see John 4:10, 13-14)? More than just another meeting to attend. More than just another Christian duty to check off. But a creating and releasing time of sharing together. Most Christian adults will respond to a Sunday School class that is free of red tape and that meets their needs. They are open to a time to study and pray and laugh and share and cry and give and live. They have had bad news all week long. Now they are more than ready for some good news.

Good news! That's what they want; that's what they desperately need. And that's exactly what we have to give—the Good News! They have some big problems that have risen in their minds, some big questions for which they urgently need some big answers. All week long they have been hyped and conned and manipulated. Now they need that welcome breath of fresh air. For adult Sunday School to happen in the 21st century, we must experience again the renewing winds of the Holy Spirit. At least three things need to happen to open us up for a time of renewal and refueling and provide us that much-needed breath of fresh air: (1) digging, (2) lifting, and (3) extending.

A Ministry of Digging

Digging means getting down deeply into the Word of God. Many of our relationships are surface relationships. The high-tech, computerized society of the 21st century may further deteriorate in-depth commitments and relationships. A majority of television programs are terribly shallow and intellectually undemanding. Howard Hendricks, a professor of

Christian education at Dallas Theological Seminary, said to one of his classes at seminary, "The problem with the average guy coming out of the unversity is that he can't read, he can't write and he can't think. And if you can't read, write or think, what can you do?" "Watch television," someone answered.[7] He might be right! Even some devotional reading is surface. God's Word does provide some answers for the big problems and big questions of our lives; but to find these answers will require digging below the surface to uncover the truth of God for my problem. The solution will not usually knock me over and force entrance into my life; but when I am able to dig deeply and get in touch with eternal truth, a lot of that which binds me and holds me captive begins to fall off. Bob Benson was a breath of fresh air to many of us who heard him speak or who read his books. His little piece called "Digging" illustrates beautifully the point I am trying to make.

God and I raised a flowerbed—He really did the most I guess because we used His soil, His air, His water, His life, His sun. My part seemed so trivial that I said, Lord, You take those bulbs and make them grow right here in the box out in the garage—You don't need me, Lord, You can do it by Yourself." "No," He said. "I want to do My part, I'm waiting to begin, but you must do yours, too. You'll have to dig the bed, bury the bulbs, pull the weeds." "Okay," I said, and I did my feeble part and God took those bulbs, burst them with life, fed them with soil, showered them with rain, drew them with sunshine, until we had beautiful flowers. And then He seemed to say, "Your life is like a garden and if you'd like, we'll make it a beautiful thing. I'll furnish the soil of grace, the sunshine of love, the rains of blessing, the wonder of life, but you must do the digging."

"Lord, You just go ahead. Make me what You want me to be—make me a saint, fill me with compassion, give me great faith." "No," He said, "you've got to keep your heart tilled, hoe the weeds of evil, chop away the second-best. I'll make you anything—pure, clean, noble, useful—anything you want to be—but only if you dig."[8]

As Benson reminds us, Jesus indicates that if we will pay

whatever price is required for us to know the truth, "the truth will set you free" (John 8:31-32). The best way to become acquainted with the Person of Truth is to become acquainted with the written Word of Truth, the Bible. Such freedom as we find in the Word is like a gentle breeze, a cool drink of water, or a breath of fresh air.

A Ministry of Lifting

Lifting occurs when believers get together around the Word. There is something unique and special about *getting together* as believers. The great temptation of the 21st century will be to *not* get together. We come together with a common focus—the Bible. We come together with a common experience —the Christian faith. The mere fact that we are here— together—brings a certain kind of inspiration or lift. I refer again to Toffler's conclusion that the emerging civilization of tomorrow will have three basic requirements for each individual: the needs for community, structure, and meaning.[9] A breath-of-fresh-air adult Sunday School class can meet all three of these requirements. Coming together with a common experience can bring community. A common focus can provide structure. The lift and inspiration come when one finds an experience to be meaningful.

Richard Foster believes that "if we value fellowship, then we should provide quiet places of beauty and color where friends can sit and visit."[10] The creators of the 21st-century church building and educational unit need to give some serious thought to the kinds of places and furnishings adults seek for times of fellowship and togetherness. We could build much more utilitarian and aesthetic facilities than we usually do for our growing adult population.

A Ministry of Extending

It is one thing to dig into the Word, another to be lifted

and inspired by the truth, but it is altogether another thing to extend the truth into the days of the weeks of your life. This is the most invigorating experience of all. You cannot dig below the surface of the Word of God without uncovering new truth, new hope, new courage. When you uncover it, it begins to gnaw away at you. It begins to clamor for embodiment. Truth is meant to be enfleshed, incarnated, lived out. Truth is most meaningful when it is lived out in somebody's life. It is not sufficient just to discover truth and be lifted by it. The whole reason for discovery is that it might be lived out in my life. As I begin to "bridge the truth" into the days of the weeks of my life, I begin to experience the rejuvenating and recreating power of the Word.

My nephew, David, was five years old last year. He became so enamored with embodying the Scripture that he asked his father to nail two boards together and make a little cross for him. He wanted to reenact the last days of Jesus. There are almost no limits to the fertile imagination of a five-year-old. One morning David had been carrying the cross and doing his thing when his father walked by. His dad came by just as David was slowly rising off the couch and out from under a large white sheet. He blew his dad away with these classic lines. "Would you please go get me some of those loaves and fishes?" he asked his startled father. "I've been in that tomb for three days, and I'm starving to death!" He obviously was taking some liberties with the Scriptures, but he was making a valiant attempt to relive that story in his own five-year-old life.

If the predictions are anywhere near correct, one of the critical needs in the 21st century will be to extend the truth and fellowship of Christian education and ministry into the home. The return home will necessitate the creation of some additional structures and delivery systems to provide activities and magazines and resources for use in the home. Here is the problem. The trend today seems to be against opening up your home. Bishop Wilke claims that his church no longer opens their homes. He believes that "the most powerful hidden resource for our church in winning new people to faith and fellowship is our homes."[11] But our sophisticated culture pushes us to make our homes to be places of privacy and refuge. We resent any intrusion. We don't want to go anywhere, and we don't want anybody intruding into "our space." Wilke believes that if 10 percent of the people of his denomination would open their homes for one night a week for Bible study and prayer and would invite newcomers into the fellowship, it would literally revolutionize the church. "People will come to our homes," he claims, "who will never, at first, come to our churches."[12] It may very well be that *the great "new" open door* for evangelism and church growth in the 21st century will be the ministry of the home. It may also be that to open one's home to such as this may be one of the toughest tests of commitment for the Christian resident of the 21st century.

There is a *time to dig* below the surface in Bible study, and a *time to lift* and encourage together; but there is also a *time to act* and a *time to speak.* To fail to act or to speak out when the time is right for acting and speaking can have critical results. Martin Niemöller describes such a time in his own life. Niemöller was a prominent Protestant minister in Germany when Hitler came to power. He writes the following account:

> In Germany, the Nazis first came for the communists, and I did not speak up because I was not a communist. Then, they came for the Jews, and I did not speak up because I was not a Jew. Then, they came for the trade unionists, and I did not speak up because I wasn't a trade unionist. Then, they came for the Catholics, and I was a Protestant, so I didn't speak up. Then they came for me. . . . By that time, there was no one to speak up for anyone![13]

The Bible study hour was meant to be a time of fellowship with our brothers and sisters. It should invigorate us like a breath of fresh air. But this is only the beginning. Living out the Word in our lives and in our homes keeps the fresh air of the Spirit flowing through our lives. "Man was meant to be a channel," writes Richard Halverson, "not a reservoir. When man shuts up the out-go in his life, he stagnates. His life gets clogged. When he lets go, opens the channel, he mellows and matures."[14]

When you begin to live out the gospel, it is almost as if the breath of God blows across your life. You begin to walk a little taller. You seem to have renewed spiritual energy. Your Christian life seems to take on new meaning and purpose. There is nothing that will energize a Christian more than to live out the gospel by investing in others. There is a new freedom in living and serving and giving. Too many of us have gotten comfortable and have forgotten the joy of serving. It all flows out of digging, lifting, and extending, and not out of grabbing or getting or accumulating. Mother Teresa of Calcutta must surely be one of the most fulfilled and joyous persons in the world—but her freedom comes as she labors endlessly among India's masses of sick and destitute people. It was recently reported that all in the world she owns are (1) her crucifix, (2) her sandals, and (3) three white cotton saris edged in blue (one for washing, one for wearing, and one for mending). None of us own that little, yet many of us are not happy, are not enjoying life, and are not fulfilled. Maybe one of the keys to personal renewal and to a renewal in our local church could be found in a program of adult Christian education that focuses on digging, lifting, and extending.

Summary

Paint a scenario of 21st-century extremes! Include in your scenario all of the most radical changes possible. Describe a world that is predominately adult, a world that is highly technological, and a world where nothing seems to be nailed down. Depict the changing roles in marriage, family, home, and workplace. Place in the middle of this futuristic scenario an adult Sunday School class. Portray what it is that these adults really need to have happen in and as a result of that meeting together. The scenario would show that these adults desperately want to know what the Bible has to say about them and their lives. And it would show that one of their greatest needs is for a breath of fresh air on the first day of the week. The wonderful thing is that fresh air is something every single Sunday School class can provide.

A breath of fresh air is usually the result of good news. We do have the choice of making the good news of the gospel or the bad news of this fallen world the focus of what we do. It is possible to plan to make the adult class a good news session—a creating, releasing, and healing time. It is also true that many times fresh air comes to us as a serendipity.

A breath of fresh air came to one of our college chapel services last year, unexpectedly. Jerry and Larra had been dating for some time, and everybody assumed he had already proposed to her. Not so! After a while, it became a kind of joke on our campus. I will never forget the way he finally did it. It was a January chapel service. The student body were gathered en masse and were waiting for the chapel service to begin. Jerry, one of our outstanding students, stood to make some announcements. He had it all prearranged, but Larra did not know. Finishing his announcements, Jerry began, "I have asked for a personal moment this morning." A hush fell across the crowd. Those who had been studying paused and looked up. "I would like to take this moment," Jerry continued, "to tell someone in this chapel service that I love her very much." You could have heard a pin drop. "Larra," he said, "I love you very much and would like to ask you to marry me." Without any prompting, a spontaneous gush of electricity swept the crowd, and in unison we all stood. Some cheered and some cried as Larra was escorted to the front to receive beautiful red roses and a kiss from her fiancé. It was electric. It was spontaneous. It was almost as if an unseen force pushed the crowd to its feet and squeezed a cheer out of them. The best way to describe its impact on that college chapel crowd is to say that it was like a breath of fresh air.

I firmly believe the Holy Spirit would be pleased to sweep across these future gatherings of adults around His Word. Like a quiet spring rain, a gentle breeze, a cool drink, or a breath of fresh air, He would come to bring meaning and healing and joy. It happened when Ezra, the teacher, stood to read to the children of Israel from the Book of the Law of Moses. Men and women had gathered together. The Word of God was the focus of their attention. The teachers "read from the Book of the Law of God, making it clear and giving the meaning so that the people could understand what was being read" (Neh. 8:8). The people were so lifted by this breath of fresh air that they bowed down and worshiped the Lord in a great celebration. Nehemiah, the governor, reminded them of something they needed to know and something we must not forget: "The joy of the Lord is your strength" (v. 10). Whether it is 400 years before Christ or the 21st century after Christ, the need of adults for "the joy of the Lord" and a breath of fresh air is still the same. We are still a pilgrim Church. We are still "just a-passin' through." We are made for two worlds, so we are tent dwellers and are ready to respond and move as God leads us. Wherever God may lead us and whatever God may ask of us, we are ready to follow Him into an exciting new day. With the unknown poet, we can say:

> *I do not know what the future holds*
> *Of joy or pain,*
> *Of loss or gain,*
> *Along life's untrod way:*
> *But I believe*
> *I can receive*
> *God's promised guidance day by day:*
> *So I securely travel on.*
>
> *And if, at times, the journey leads*
> *Through waters deep*
> *Or mountains steep,*
> *I know this unseen Friend,*
> *His love revealing,*
> *His presence healing,*
> *Walks with me to the journey's end;*
> *So I securely travel on.* [15]

Let's join together and, with the help of the Holy Spirit, shape a wonderful, new tomorrow for the Christian education of adults!

Notes

INTRODUCTION

1. Richard Wilke, *And Are We Yet Alive?* (Nashville: Abingdon Press, 1986), 10-11.

2. Ibid.

3. *Sky,* June 1988, 48. Delta Airlines magazine.

4. Connie Leslie, "The Graying of the Campus," *Newsweek,* June 6, 1988, 56.

5. John Stott, *The Year 2000* (Downers Grove, Ill.: InterVarsity Press, 1983), viii.

6. John Gardner, *Self-Renewal* (New York: W. W. Norton & Co., 1981), 106.

7. George Roche, *A World Without Heroes* (Hillsdale, Mich.: Hillsdale College Press, 1987), 346.

CHAPTER 1

1. Alvin Toffler, *The Third Wave* (New York: Bantam Books, 1981), 70.

2. Ibid., 21.

3. Ibid., 28.

4. Ibid., 61.

5. Ibid., 1.

6. Patricia Cross, "Adult Education in the Twenty-first Century," *Journal of Adult Training,* Fall 1988, 5.

7. Toffler, *Third Wave,* 124.

8. Ibid., 235.

9. Bureau of the Census, *Population Estimates and Projections* (Washington, D.C., October, 1982), 1.

10. John Stott, *Involvement: Social and Sexual Relationships in the Modern World* (Old Tappan, N.J.: Fleming H. Revell Co., 1985), foreword.

11. Jerry Stubblefield, *A Church Ministering to Adults* (Nashville: Broadman Press, 1986), 278.

12. See n. 9.

13. Ledford Bischof, *Adult Psychology* (New York: Harper & Row, Publishers, 1976), 308.

14. Cheryl Russell, *100 Predictions for the Baby Boom: The Next 50 Years* (New York: Plenum Press, 1987), 15-17.

15. Ibid.

16. Ibid.

17. See n. 9.

18. See n. 11.

19. Paul Loth, "Christian Adult Training in the Years Ahead," *Journal of Adult Training,* Fall 1988, 2.

20. Charles Swindoll, *Come Before Winter* (Portland, Oreg.: Multnomah Press, 1985), 26-27.

21. Toffler, *Third Wave,* 194, 203.

22. Russell, *Predictions,* 17.

23. Ibid., 134.

24. Ibid., 135.

25. Toffler, *Third Wave,* 196-97.

26. Russell, *Predictions,* 55-56.

27. Toffler, *Third Wave,* 219.

28. Ibid., 212.

29. Ibid., 221.

30. Russell, *Predictions,* 108.

31. Ibid., 122.

32. Ibid., 92, 105.

33. Toffler, *Third Wave,* 214.

34. Ibid., 212.

35. Stott, *Involvement,* 19.

36. Ibid., 22.

37. William Johnson, *Workforce 2000* (Indianapolis: Hudson Institute, 1987), xiii.

38. Russell, *Predictions,* 76.

39. Ibid., 138.

40. Ibid., 154.

41. Harvey Cox, *Religion in the Secular City: Toward a Post-Modern Theology* (New York: Simon & Schuster, 1984), 11.

42. Ibid., 14.

43. Richard Ostling, "Giddy Days for the Russian Church," *Time,* June 20, 1988, 57-58.

44. Eric Bridges, "Freer but Fragile: The Church in China," *Christianity Today,* April 22, 1988, 44-45.

45. Toffler, *Third Wave,* 289.

46. "Poll Says Religion Belongs in Public Life," *Christianity Today,* March 4, 1988, 38.

47. Richard Ostling, "Americans Facing Toward Mecca," *Time,* May 23, 1988, 49-50.

CHAPTER 2

1. Arnold Toynbee, *Surviving the Future* (London: Oxford University Press, 1971), 95.

2. Tom Driver, "Theology of Culture," *Religious Education,* Spring 1987, 267.

3. Malcomb Scully, *The Chronicle of Higher Education,* January 21, 1974; in Marvin Taylor, *Foundations for Christian Education* (Nashville: Abingdon Press, 1976), 17.

4. Charles Colson, *Who Speaks for God?* (Westchester, Ill.: Crossway Books, 1985), 128.

5. Roche, *Heroes,* 2.

6. Wilke, *Alive?* 114-15.

7. Charles Swindoll, *Come Before Winter,* 211-12.

8. Colson, *Who Speaks for God?* 96.

9. See n. 2.

10. Herbert Schlossberg, *Idols for Destruction* (Nashville: Thomas Nelson Publishers, 1983), 39-40.

11. Cox, *Religion,* 42.

12. Colson, *Who Speaks for God?* 36.

13. Robert Banks, *The Tyranny of Time* (Downers Grove, Ill.: InterVarsity Press, 1983), 21.

14. Ibid., 22.

15. Henry David Thoreau, "Where I Lived, and What I Lived For," in *Walden* (New York: Library of America, 1985), 394.

16. Ibid., 395.

17. Wilke, *Alive?* 103.

18. "Report of the Study Commission on Theology, Education, and the Electronic Media," *Religious Education,* Spring 1987, 169.

19. Ibid.

20. Colson, *Who Speaks for God?* 95.

21. Schlossberg, *Idols,* 254.

22. Hans Kung, *On Being a Christian* (London: Collings, 1976), 57.

23. Charles Allen, *The Miracle of Love* (New York: Fleming H. Revell Co., 1972), 18-19.

24. Schlossberg, *Idols,* 238.

25. Gardner, *Self-Renewal,* xxi.

26. Charles Stanley, *Confronting Casual Christianity* (Nashville: Broadman Press, 1985), 11.

27. Richard Niebuhr, *Christ and Culture* (New York: Harper & Row, Publishers, 1951). These themes are dealt with throughout the book.

CHAPTER 3

1. W. T. Purkiser, Richard S. Taylor, and Willard H. Taylor, *God, Man, and Salvation* (Kansas City: Beacon Hill Press of Kansas City, 1977), 13.

2. Schlossberg, *Idols,* 164.

3. Gardner, *Self-Renewal,* 100-101.

4. Henri Nouwen, *Reaching Out* (Garden City, N.Y.: Image Books, 1975), 73.

5. Colson, *Who Speaks for God?* 151.

6. Thoreau, "Where I Lived," 392.

7. Colson, *Who Speaks for God?* 188.

8. Russell, *Predictions,* 190.

9. Schlossberg, *Idols,* 78.

10. Gardner, *Self-Renewal,* 13.

11. Ibid., 14.

12. Nouwen, *Reaching Out,* 34.

13. Ken Chafin, *Is There a Family in the House?* (Waco, Tex.: Word Books, 1978), 15, 16, 18.

14. Ross Snyder, "Worship as Celebration and Nurture," in *Foundations for Christian Education* (Nashville: Abingdon Press, 1976), 176.

15. Nouwen, *Reaching Out,* 113.

16. Ibid., 126-27.

17. Stott, *Year 2000,* viii-ix.

18. James Fowler, *Becoming Adult, Becoming Christian* (San Francisco: Harper & Row, Publishers, 1984), 1.

19. Bischof, *Adult Psychology,* 217.

20. Bob Benson, *In Quest of Shared Life* (Nashville: Impact Books, 1981), 87.

21. Gordon MacDonald, *Ordering Your Private World* (Nashville: Thomas Nelson Publishers, 1985), 107.

22. Tim Hansel, *Holy Sweat* (Waco, Tex.: Word Books, 1987), 25.

23. Hannah Whitall Smith, *The Christian's Secret of a Happy Life* (Old Tappan, N.J.: Fleming H. Revell Co., 1968), 116.

24. Richard Olson, *Mid-Life: A Time to Discover, a Time to Decide* (Valley Forge, Pa.: Judson Press, 1980), 140.

25. Ibid., 146-47.

26. Snyder, "Worship," 176.

27. Toffler, *Third Wave,* 367.

28. Cox, *Religion,* 159.

CHAPTER 4

1. Charles Swindoll, *Growing Deep in the Christian Life: Returning to Our Roots* (Portland, Oreg.: Multnomah Press, 1986), 389.

2. Ibid., 390.

3. MacDonald, *Ordering,* 127.

4. Ibid., 145.

5. Russell Dilday, "From the President," *Southwestern News,* March 1988, 2.

6. F. F. Bruce, *Commentary on the Book of Acts* (Grand Rapids: Wm. B. Eerdmans Publishing Co., 1954), 39.

7. G. Campbell Morgan, *The Acts of the Apostles* (Westwood, N.J.: Fleming H. Revell Co., 1924), 166.

8. Wilke, *Alive?* 89.

9. Ibid.

10. Ibid., 85.

11. Raymond Studzinski, *Spiritual Direction and Mid-Life Development* (Chicago: Loyola University Press, 1985), 122; quoted from "Sayings of Light and Love," in *The Collected Works of St. John of the Cross.*

12. Bob Benson and Michael Benson, *Disciplines for the Inner Life* (Waco, Tex.: Word Books, 1985), 103. A poem by Norman Nash.

13. Colson, *Who Speaks for God?* 24, 33.

14. Bruce, *Acts,* 84.

15. Allen, *Miracle of Love,* 20.

CHAPTER 5

1. Dick Murray, *Strengthening the Adult Sunday School Class* (Nashville: Abingdon Press, 1981), 79.

2. Ibid., 64.

3. Lyle Schaller, *Hey, That's Our Church!* (Nashville: Abingdon Press, 1975), 108.

4. Stubblefield, *Ministering,* 298.

5. Murray, *Strengthening,* 81.

6. Swindoll, *Growing Deep,* 375.

7. Murray, *Strengthening,* 78.

8. Ibid., 28-29.

9. George Hunter III, *To Spread the Power* (Nashville: Abingdon Press, 1987), 186.

CHAPTER 6

1. F. Davidson, *The New Bible Commentary* (Grand Rapids: Wm. B. Eerdmans Publishing Co., 1963), 78.

2. Swindoll, *Growing Deep,* 398.

3. John Killinger, *Christ in the Seasons of Ministry* (Waco, Tex.: Word Books, 1981), 53.

4. Os Guinness, *The Dust of Death* (Downers Grove, Ill.: InterVarsity Press, 1975), 277.

5. MacDonald, *Ordering,* 40.

6. Wilke, *Alive?* 29.

7. Howard Hendricks, *Teaching to Change Lives* (Portland, Oreg.: Multnomah Press, 1987), 54.

8. Bob Benson, *Laughter in the Walls* (Nashville: Impact Books, 1969), 74-75.

9. Toffler, *Third Wave,* 367.

10. Richard Foster, *Freedom of Simplicity* (San Francisco: Harper & Row, Publishers, 1981), 154.

11. Wilke, *Alive?* 81.

12. Ibid., 82.

13. Charles Allen, *Perfect Peace* (New York: Fleming H. Revell Co., 1979), 102.

14. Richard Halverson, *Between Sundays* (Grand Rapids: Zondervan Publishing House, 1965), 68.

15. Charles Allen, *You Are Never Alone* (Old Tappan, N.J.: Fleming H. Revell Co., 1978), 157.